THE COLEMAN COLLECTION

A COLLECTION

OF THE

Facts and *Documents*, relative to the *Death* of MAJOR - GENERAL

Alexander Hamilton;

With Comments: Together with the various *Orations*, *Sermons*, and *Eulogies*, that have been Published or Written on his *Life* and *Character*.

> Quoad humanum genus incolume manserit, quamdiu usus literis, honor summæ eloquentiæ pretium erit, quamdiu rerum natura aut fortuna steterit, aut memoria duraverit, admirabile, posteris vigebis ingenium. — AURELIUS FUSCUS.

By the Editor of The Evening Post.

Select Bibliographies Reprint Series

BOOKS FOR LIBRARIES PRESS
FREEPORT, NEW YORK

This Edition First Published 1904
Reprinted 1969

E302.6
H2 C6

STANDARD BOOK NUMBER:
8369-5025-9

LIBRARY OF CONGRESS CATALOG CARD NUMBER:
72-95068

PRINTED IN THE UNITED STATES OF AMERICA

NOTE TO ORIGINAL EDITION

It is precisely one hundred years since American citizens were shocked by the tragic fate of Alexander Hamilton. The country has many times been called upon to mourn the violent death of her public men; but scarcely the wanton assassinations of Lincoln, Garfield, and McKinley have moved Americans to more poignant sorrow than was caused by the intelligence that General Hamilton, in the forty-eighth year of his age, and in the fullness of a great career, had been shot in a duel with Aaron Burr, then Vice-President of the United States, on July 11, 1804.

The rare volume which is here reprinted preserves the record of the contemporary impression made by this most famous duel in our political annals. It was prepared by William Coleman, a native of Massachusetts, who had removed to New York city about 1794, and was for a brief period the law partner of Aaron Burr. When Hamilton and other gentlemen desired to found a new Federalist daily in 1801, they turned to Coleman, who thus became the first editor of the New York "Evening Post," which he conducted with distinction until his death in 1829. A party associate and personal friend of Hamilton, and knowing well also the character and motives of Burr, Coleman desired to make a permanent memorial of the circumstances which led to the duel, the details of the affair itself, and the various eulogies called forth throughout the country by Hamilton's untimely death. He performed his task with dignity and taste, and the volume affords an excellent opportunity to study the manifestation of American popular feeling, through the press and by means of public assemblies, at the opening of the nineteenth century.

Nothing in the volume is so justly famous, however, as the remarkable memorial address delivered in Albany by Eliphalet Nott, then a clergyman of but thirty-one years of age, and destined to assume, in that very year, the presidency of Union College. This oration, by reason of its moving eloquence and the courage with which it attacked the institution of dueling, gave its author immediately a national reputation. For fifty years after its delivery, few examples of pulpit oratory were more frequently drawn upon in extracts for the use of school Readers and Speakers. It thus became known by a few brilliant paragraphs only, and there are not many Americans of the present generation who have read the noble address in its entirety.

For the suggestion of reprinting this curious and interesting volume, the publishers are indebted to the friendly service of George Franklin Seymour, Bishop of Springfield, Illinois, who has also kindly allowed them to make use of his own copy of the original issue of 1804, now most difficult to procure.

4 PARK STREET, 1904.

PREFACE.

THIS *Collection of Papers*, and the comments and remarks which will occasionally accompany them, are offered to the public no less in gratification of my own feelings, than in compliance with the request of those whose wishes I have long been accustomed to respect.

IN the death of HAMILTON, I have lost my best earthly friend, my ablest adviser, and my most generous and disinterested patron. And all that is now left me, is to pour forth my gratitude in unavailing sorrow; and to evince my regard for his memory, by defending it against the cruel attacks of those, who, not contented with having deprived him of his life, seem bent on pursuing him beyond the grave, and destroying his fame. A belief is confidently indulged, that when this series of Numbers shall be completed, enough will have appeared to silence the voice of calumny forever.

THIS Collection will contain all the documents and publications, which, it is presumed, the friends of General HAMILTON would wish to see preserved in a more permanent form than that of a Gazette. Most of the papers and facts have, indeed, already appeared; but some things of a very interesting nature are now for the first time published; and the remarks on the Correspondence and circumstances connected with the fatal event, will be found to have been materially revised, corrected, and methodized, since their first hasty appearance in the Evening Post.

A COLLECTION, &c.

———✿———

In the following pages will be found a satisfactory account of the shocking catastrophe which has deprived America of her most valuable citizen, and our age of the greatest man; together with some brief remarks, calculated to place the melancholy affair in its true light, both as it respects the deceased, and him by whose arm he was slain.

Perhaps the most satisfactory manner of introducing the reader to his subject, will be to begin with the Correspondence which led to the fatal interview. It follows:

N°. I.

New-York, June 18, 1804.

Sir,

I send for your perusal a letter signed Charles D. Cooper, which, though apparently published some time ago, has but very recently come to my knowledge. Mr. Van Ness, who does me the favour to deliver this, will point out to you that clause of the letter to which I particularly request your attention.

You must perceive, Sir, the necessity of a prompt and unqualified acknowledgment or denial of the use of any expression which would warrant the assertions of Dr. Cooper.

I have the honour to be,
Your obedient serv't,
A. BURR.

General HAMILTON.

N°. II.

New-York, June 20, 1804.

SIR,

I HAVE maturely reflected on the subject of your letter of the 18th inst. and the more I have reflected the more I have become convinced, that I could not, without manifest impropriety, make the avowal or disavowal which you seem to think necessary. The clause pointed out by Mr. Van Ness is in these terms : " I could detail to you a *still more despicable* opinion which General Hamilton *has expressed* of Mr. Burr." To endeavour to discover the meaning of this declaration, I was obliged to seek in the antecedent part of this letter for the opinion to which it referred, as having been already disclosed. I found it in these words : " General Hamilton and Judge Kent have declared in *substance*, that they looked upon Mr. Burr to be a *dangerous man*, and one *who ought not to be trusted with the reins of government.*"

THE language of Dr. Cooper plainly implies, that *he* considered this opinion of you, which he attributes to me, as a *despicable* one ; but he affirms that I have expressed some other, *more despicable*, without, however, mentioning to whom, when, or where. 'T is evident that the phrase, " still more despicable," admits of infinite shades, from very light to very dark. How am I to judge of the degree intended? or how shall I annex any precise idea to language so indefinite?

BETWEEN gentlemen, *despicable* and *more despicable* are not worth the pains of distinction: when therefore you do not interrogate me, as to the opinion which is specifically ascribed to me, I must conclude, that you view it as within the limits to which the animadversions of political opponents upon each other may justifiably extend, and consequently as not warranting the idea of it which Doctor Cooper appears to entertain. If so, what precise inference could you draw, as a guide for your conduct, were I to acknowledge that I had expressed an opinion of you *still more despicable* than the one which is particularized? How could you be sure that even this opinion had exceeded the bounds which you would yourself deem admissible between political opponents?

BUT I forbear further comment on the embarrassment, to which the requisition you have made naturally leads. The occasion forbids a more ample illustration, though nothing could be more easy than to pursue it.

REPEATING that I cannot reconcile it with propriety to make the acknowledgment or denial you desire, I will add that I deem it inadmissible on principle, to consent to be interrogated as to the justness of the *inferences* which may be drawn by others from whatever I may have said of a political opponent, in the course of fifteen years competition. If there were no other objection to it this is sufficient, that it would tend to expose my sincerity and delicacy to injurious imputations from every person who may at any time have conceived the *import* of my expressions, differently from what I may then have intended or may afterwards recollect. I stand ready to avow or disavow promptly and explicitly any precise or definite opinion which I may be charged with having declared of any Gentleman. More than this cannot fitly be expected from me; and especially it cannot be reasonably expected that I shall enter into an explanation upon a basis so vague as that which you have adopted. I trust on more reflection you will see the matter in the same light with me. If not, I can only regret the circumstance and must abide the consequences.

THE publication of Doctor Cooper was never seen by me till after the receipt of your letter.

I have the honour to be, &c.
A. HAMILTON.

Col. BURR.

N°. III.

New-York, 21st June, 1804.

SIR,

YOUR letter of the 20th instant has been this day received. Having considered it attentively, I regret to find in it nothing of that sincerity and delicacy which you profess to value.

POLITICAL opposition can never absolve gentlemen from the necessity of a rigid adherence to the laws of honour, and the rules of decorum. I neither claim such privilege nor indulge it in others.

THE common sense of mankind affixes to the epithet adopted by Dr. Cooper, the idea of dishonour. It has been publicly applied to me under the sanction of your name. The question is not, whether he has understood the meaning of the word, or has used it according to syntax, and with grammatical accuracy; but, whether you have authorized this application, either directly or by uttering expressions or opinions derogatory to my honour. The time "when" is in your own knowledge, but no way material to me, as the calumny has now first been disclosed, so as to become the subject of my notice, and as the effect is present and palpable.

Your letter has furnished me with new reasons for requiring a definite reply.

> I have the honour to be,
> Sir, your obedient,
> A. BURR.

General Hamilton.

On Saturday the 22d of June, General Hamilton, for the first time, called on Mr. Pendleton and communicated to him the preceding correspondence. He informed him that in a conversation with Mr. Van Ness at the time of receiving the last letter, he told Mr. Van Ness that he considered that letter as rude and offensive, and that it was not possible for him to give it any other answer than that Mr. Burr must take such steps as he might think proper. He said farther, that Mr. Van Ness requested him to take time to deliberate, and then return an answer, when he might possibly entertain a different opinion, and that he would call on him to receive it. That his reply to Mr. Van Ness was, that he did not perceive it possible for him to give any other answer than that he had mentioned, unless Mr. Burr would take back his last letter and write one which would admit of a different reply. He then gave Mr. Pendleton the letter hereafter mentioned of the 22d of June, to be delivered to Mr. Van Ness when he should call on Mr. Pendleton for an answer, and went to his country house.

THE next day General Hamilton received, while there, the following letter.

N°. IV.

June 23d, 1804.

SIR,

IN the afternoon of yesterday, I reported to Col. Burr the result of my last interview with you, and appointed the evening to receive his further instructions. Some private engagements, however, prevented me from calling on him till this morning. On my return to the city, I found upon inquiry, both at your office and house, that you had returned to your residence in the country. Lest an interview there might be less agreeable to you than elsewhere, I have taken the liberty of addressing you this note to inquire when and where it will be most convenient to you to receive a communication.

Your most obedient and very humble servant,
W. P. VAN NESS.
General HAMILTON.

MR. PENDLETON understood from General Hamilton that he immediately answered, that if the communication was pressing he would receive it at his country house that day; if not, he would be at his house in town the next morning at nine o'clock. But he did not give Mr. Pendleton any copy of this note.

N°. V.

New-York, June 22, 1804.

Sir,

Your first letter, in a style too peremptory, made a demand, in my opinion, unprecedented and unwarrantable. My answer, pointing out the embarrassment, gave you an opportunity to take a less exceptionable course. You have not chosen to do it; but by your last letter received this day, containing expressions *indecorous* and improper, you have increased the difficulties to explanation intrinsically incident to the nature of your application.

If by a " definite reply," you mean the direct avowal or disavowal required in your first letter, I have no other answer to give, than that which has already been given. If you mean anything different, admitting of greater latitude, it is requisite you should explain.

I have the honour to be,
Sir, your obedient servant,
ALEX. HAMILTON.

Aaron Burr, Esq.

This letter, although dated on the 22d June, remained in Mr. Pendleton's possession until the 25th, within which period he had several conversations with Mr. Van Ness. In these conversations Mr. Pendleton endeavoured to illustrate and enforce the propriety of the ground General Hamilton had taken. Mr. Pendleton mentioned to Mr. Van Ness as the result, that if Col. Burr would write a letter, requesting to know in substance whether in the conversation to which Dr. Cooper alluded, any particular instance of dishonourable conduct was imputed to Col. Burr, or whether there was any impeachment of his private character, Gen. Hamilton would declare to the best of his recollection what passed in that conversation : and Mr. Pendleton read to Mr. Van Ness a paper containing the substance of what Gen. Hamilton would say on that subject, which is as follows.

N°. VI.

" GENERAL HAMILTON says he cannot imagine to what Dr. Cooper may have alluded, unless it were to a conversation at Mr. Taylor's in Albany, last winter, (at which he and Gen. Hamilton were present). Gen. Hamilton cannot recollect distinctly the particulars of that conversation so as to undertake to repeat them, without running the risk of varying, or omitting what might be deemed important circumstances. The expressions are entirely forgotten, and the specific ideas imperfectly remembered ; but to the best of his recollection it consisted of comments on the political principles and views of Col. Burr, and the results that might be expected from them in the event of his election as Governor, without reference to any particular instance of past conduct, or to private character."

AFTER the delivery of the letter of the 22d, as above mentioned ; in another interview with Mr. Van Ness he desired Mr. Pendleton to give him *in writing* the substance of what he had proposed on the part of General Hamilton, which Mr. Pendleton did in the words following.

Nº. VII.

"In answer to a letter properly adapted to obtain from General Hamilton a declaration whether he had charged Col. Burr with any particular instance of dishonourable conduct, or had impeached his private character, either in the conversation alluded to by Dr. Cooper, or in any other particular instance to be specified; he would be able to answer consistently with his honour, and the truth, in substance, that the conversation to which Dr. Cooper alluded, turned wholly on political topics, and did not attribute to Col. Burr any instance of dishonourable conduct, nor relate to his private character; and in relation to any other language or conversation of General Hamilton which Col. Burr will specify, a prompt and frank avowal or denial will be given."

On the 26th June Mr. Pendleton received the following letter.

Nº. VIII.

Sir,

The letter which you yesterday delivered me, and your subsequent communication, in Col. Burr's opinion, evince no disposition on the part of Gen. Hamilton to come to a satisfactory accommodation. The injury complained of and the reparation expected, are so definitely expressed in Col. Burr's letter of the 21st instant, that there is not perceived a necessity for further explanation on his part. The difficulty that would result from confining the inquiry to any particular times and occasions must be manifest. The denial of a specified conversation only, would leave strong implications that on other occasions improper language had been used. When and where injurious opinions and expressions have been uttered by Gen. Hamilton must be best known to him, and of him only will Col. Burr inquire. *No denial or declaration will be satisfactory, unless it be general, so as wholly to exclude the idea that rumours derogatory to Colonel Burr's honour have originated with General Hamilton, or have been* fairly *inferred from any thing he has said.* A definite reply to a requisition of this nature was demanded by Col. Burr's letter of the 21st instant. This being refused, invites the alternative alluded to in Gen. Hamilton's letter of the 20th.

It was required by the position in which the controversy was placed by Gen. Hamilton on Friday[1] last, and I was immediately furnished with a communication demanding a personal interview. The necessity of this measure has not, in the opinion of Col. Burr, been diminished by the General's last letter, or any communication which has since been received. I am consequently again instructed to deliver you a message, as soon as it may be convenient for you to receive it. I beg therefore you will be so good as to inform me at what hour I can have the pleasure of seeing you.

Your most obedient, and
very humble servant,
W. P. VAN NESS.

Nathaniel Pendleton, Esq.
June 26th.

[1] June 22d.

N°. IX.

26th *June*, 1804.

Sir,

I have communicated the letter which you did me the honour to write to me of this date, to Gen. Hamilton. The expectations now disclosed on the part of Col. Burr appear to him to have greatly extended the original ground of inquiry, and instead of presenting a particular and definite case for explanation, seem to aim at nothing less than an inquisition into his most confidential conversations, as well as others, through the whole period of his acquaintance with Col. Burr.

While he was prepared to meet the particular case fairly and fully, he thinks it inadmissible that he should be expected to answer at large as to every thing that he may possibly have said, in relation to the character of Col. Burr, at any time or upon any occasion. Though he is not conscious that any charges which are in circulation to the prejudice of Col. Burr have originated with him, except one which may have been so considered, and which has long since been fully explained between Col. Burr and himself — yet he cannot consent to be questioned generally as to any *rumours* which may be afloat derogatory to the character of Col. Burr, without specification of the several rumours, many of them probably unknown to him. He does not, however, mean to authorize any conclusion as to the real nature of his conduct in relation to Col. Burr, by his declining so loose and vague a basis of explanation, and he disavows an unwillingness to come to a satisfactory, provided it be an honourable, accommodation. His objection is, the very indefinite ground which Col. Burr has assumed, in which he is sorry to be able to discern nothing short of predetermined hostility. Presuming therefore that it will be adhered to, he has instructed me to receive the message which you have it in charge to deliver. For this purpose I shall be at home and at your command to-morrow morning from eight to ten o'clock.

I have the honour to be, respectfully,
Your obedient servant,
NATHANIEL PENDLETON.

WILLIAM P. VAN NESS, Esq.

N°. X.

SIR,

THE letter which I had the honour to receive from you, under date of yesterday, states, among other things, that in Gen. Hamilton's opinion, Col. Burr has taken a very indefinite ground, in which he evinces nothing short of predetermined hostility, and that Gen. Hamilton thinks it inadmissible that the inquiry should extend to his confidential as well as other conversations. In this Col. Burr can only reply, that secret whispers traducing his fame, and impeaching his honour, are, at least, equally injurious with slanders publicly uttered; that Gen. Hamilton had, at no time, and in no place, a right to use any such injurious expressions; and that the partial negative he is disposed to give, with the reservations he wishes to make, are proofs that he has done the injury specified.

COL. BURR'S request was, in the first instance, proposed in a form the most simple, in order that Gen. Hamilton might give to the affair that course to which he might be induced by his temper and his knowledge of facts. Col. Burr trusted with confidence, that from the frankness of a soldier and the candour of a gentleman, he might expect an ingenuous declaration. That if, as he had reason to believe, Gen. Hamilton had used expressions derogatory to his honour, he would have had the magnanimity to retract them; and that if, from his language, injurious inferences had been improperly drawn, he would have perceived the propriety of correcting errors, which might thus have been widely diffused. With these impressions, Col. Burr was greatly surprised at receiving a letter which he considered as evasive, and which in manner he deemed not altogether decorous. In one expectation, however, he was not wholly deceived, for the close of Gen. Hamilton's letter contained an intimation that if Col. Burr should dislike his refusal to acknowledge or deny, he was ready to meet the consequences. This Col. Burr deemed a sort of defiance, and would have felt justified in making it the basis of an immediate message. But as the communication contained something concerning the indefiniteness of the request; as he believed it rather the offspring of false pride than of reflection, and as he felt the utmost reluctance to proceed to extremities, while any other hope remained, his request was repeated in terms more explicit. The replies and propositions on the part of Gen. Hamilton have, in Col. Burr's opinion, been constantly in substance the same.

Col. Burr disavows all motives of predetermined hostility, a charge by which he thinks insult added to injury. He feels as a gentleman should feel when his honour is impeached or assailed; and without sensations of hostility or wishes of revenge, he is determined to vindicate that honour at such hazard as the nature of the case demands.

THE length to which this correspondence has extended, only tending to prove that the satisfactory redress, earnestly desired, cannot be obtained, he deems it useless to offer any proposition except the simple message which I shall now have the honour to deliver.

I have the honour to be with great respect,
Your obedient and very humble servant,
W. P. VAN NESS.
Wednesday Morning, June 27th, 1804.

WITH this letter a message was received, such as was to be expected, containing an invitation which was accepted, and Mr. Pendleton informed Mr. Van Ness he should hear from him the next day as to further particulars.

THIS letter was delivered to General Hamilton on the same evening, and a very short conversation ensued between him and Mr. Pendleton, who was to call on him early the next morning for a further conference. — When he did so, Gen. Hamilton said he had not understood whether the message and answer was definitively concluded, or whether another meeting was to take place for that purpose between Mr. Pendleton and Mr. Van Ness. Under the latter impression, and as the last letter contained matter that naturally led to animadversion, he gave Mr. Pendleton a paper of remarks in his own hand writing, to be communicated to Mr. Van Ness, if the state of the affair rendered it proper.

In an interview with Mr. Van Ness on the same day, after explaining the causes which had induced Gen. Hamilton to suppose that the state of the affair did not render it improper, Mr. Pendleton offered this paper to Mr. Van Ness; but he declined receiving it, alleging, that he considered the correspondence as closed by the acceptance of the message that he had delivered.

Mr. Pendleton then informed Mr. Van Ness of the inducements mentioned by Gen. Hamilton in the paper, for at least postponing the meeting until the close of the Circuit; and as this was uncertain, Mr. Pendleton was to let him know when it would be convenient.

Here we think it most proper to introduce the paper itself. The reader will form his own judgment whether it was not Mr. Van Ness's duty to have received it, and shown it to his principal; he will probably exercise his own conjecture too as to Mr. Van Ness's motives for not doing so. It follows:

N°. XI.

"*Remarks on the letter of June 27, 1804.*

"Whether the observations on this letter are designed merely to justify the result which is indicated in the close of the letter, or may be intended to give an opening for rendering any thing explicit which may have been deemed vague heretofore, can only be judged of by the sequel. At any rate it appears to me necessary not to be misunderstood. Mr. Pendleton is therefore authorized to say, that in the course of the present discussion, written or verbal, there has been no intention to evade, defy, or insult, but a sincere disposition to avoid extremities if it could be done with propriety. With this view, Gen. Hamilton has been ready to enter into a frank and free explanation on any and every object of a specific nature; but not to answer a general and abstract inquiry, embracing a period too long for any accurate recollection, and exposing him to unpleasant criticisms from, or unpleasant discussions with, any and every person, who may have understood him in an unfavourable sense. This (admitting that he could answer in a manner the most satisfactory to Col. Burr) he should deem inadmissible, in principle and precedent, and humiliating in practice. To this therefore he can never submit. Frequent allusion has been made to slanders said to be in circulation. Whether they are openly or in whispers, they have a form and shape, and might be specified.

"IF the alternative alluded to in the close of the letter is definitively tendered, it must be accepted; the time, place, and manner, to be afterwards regulated. I should not think it right in the midst of a Circuit Court to withdraw my services from those who may have confided important interests to me, and expose them to the embarrassment of seeking other counsel, who may not have time to be sufficiently instructed in their causes. I shall also want a little time to make some arrangements respecting my own affairs."

ON Friday the 6th of July, the circuit being closed, Mr. Pendleton informed Mr. Van Ness that General Hamilton would be ready at any time after the Sunday following. On Monday the particulars were arranged — on Wednesday the parties met at Weahawk, on the Jersey shore, at 7 o'clock, A. M. — The particulars of what then took place will appear from the following statement, as agreed upon and corrected by the seconds of the parties.

"COL. BURR arrived first on the ground, as had been previously agreed : when Gen. Hamilton arrived the parties exchanged salutations, and the seconds proceeded to make their arrangements. They measured the distance, ten full paces, and cast lots for the choice of position, as also to determine by whom the word should be given, both of which fell to the second of Gen. Hamilton. They then proceeded to load the pistols in each other's presence, after which the parties took their stations. The gentleman who was to give the word, then explained to the parties the rules which were to govern them in firing, which were as follows : ' The parties being placed at their stations . . . the second who gives the word shall ask them whether they are ready ; being answered in the affirmative, he shall say " *Present !* " after this the parties shall present and fire *when they please.* . . . If one fires before the other, the opposite second shall say one, two, three, fire . . . and he shall then fire or lose his fire.' He then asked if they were prepared ; being answered in the affirmative, he gave the word *present,* as had been agreed on, and both parties presented and fired in succession — the intervening time is not expressed, as the seconds do not precisely agree on that point. The fire of Colonel Burr took effect, and General Hamilton almost instantly fell. Col. Burr then advanced toward General Hamilton, with a manner and gesture that appeared to General Hamilton's friend to be expressive of regret, but without speaking, turned about and withdrew, being urged from the field by his friend as has been subsequently stated, with a view to prevent his being recognized by the surgeon and bargemen, who were then approaching. No further communication took place between the principals, and the barge that carried Col. Burr immediately returned to the city. We conceive it proper to add that the conduct of the parties in this interview was perfectly proper as suited the occasion."

THE above is a statement of only such leading particulars as the seconds supposed it would be proper for them, as such, to publish : but as I think a deep interest will be felt in every circumstance attending the death of General HAMILTON, I have been at some pains to collect all the information on the subject that was to be had from authentic sources.

IT was nearly seven in the morning when the boat which carried General Hamilton, his friend Mr. Pendleton, and the Surgeon mutually agreed on, Doctor Hosack, reached that part of the Jersey shore called the *Weahawk*. There they found Mr. Burr and his friend Mr. Van Ness, who, as I am told, had been employed since their arrival, with coats off, in clearing away the bushes, limbs of trees, &c. so as to make a fair opening. The parties in a few moments were at their allotted situations : when Mr. Pendleton gave the word, Mr. Burr raised his arm slowly, deliberately took his aim, and fired. His ball entered General Hamilton's right side : as soon as the bullet struck him, he raised himself involuntarily on his toes, turned a little to the left (at which moment his pistol went off,) and fell upon his face. Mr. Pendleton immediately called out for Dr. Hosack, who, in running to the spot, had to pass Mr. Van Ness and Col. Burr; but Van Ness had the cool precaution to cover his principal with an umbrella, so that Dr. Hosack should not be able to swear that he saw him on the field. What passed after this the reader will have in the following letter from Dr. Hosack himself, in answer to my note:

"*August* 17*th*, 1804.

"DEAR SIR,

"To comply with your request is a painful task; but I will repress my feelings while I endeavour to furnish you with an enumeration of such particulars relative to the melancholy end of our beloved friend Hamilton, as dwell most forcibly on my recollection.

"WHEN called to him, upon his receiving the fatal wound, I found him half sitting on the ground, supported in the arms of Mr. Pendleton. His countenance of death I shall never forget — He had at that instant just strength to say, 'This is a mortal wound, Doctor;' when he sunk away, and became to all appearance lifeless. I immediately stripped up his clothes, and soon, alas! ascertained that the direction of the ball must have been through some vital part.[1] His pulses were not to be felt; his respiration was entirely suspended; and upon laying my hand on his heart, and perceiving no motion there, I considered him as irrecoverably gone. I however observed to Mr. Pendleton, that the only chance for his

[1] For the satisfaction of some of General Hamilton's friends, I examined his body after death, in presence of Dr. Post and two other gentlemen. I discovered that the ball struck the second or third false rib, and fractured it about in the middle; it then passed through the liver and diaphragm, and, as nearly as we could ascertain without a minute examination, lodged in the first or second lumbar vertebra. The vertebra in which it was lodged was considerably splintered, so that the spiculæ were distinctly perceptible to the finger. About a pint of clotted blood was found in the cavity of the belly, which had probably been effused from the divided vessels of the liver.

reviving was immediately to get him upon the water. We therefore lifted him up, and carried him out of the wood, to the margin of the bank, where the bargemen aided us in conveying him into the boat, which immediately put off. During all this time I could not discover the least symptom of returning life. I now rubbed his face, lips, and temples, with spirits of hartshorne, applied it to his neck and breast, and to the wrists and palms of his hands, and endeavoured to pour some into his mouth. When we had got, as I should judge, about 50 yards from the shore, some imperfect efforts to breathe were for the first time manifest: in a few minutes he sighed, and became sensible to the impression of the hartshorne, or the fresh air of the water: He breathed; his eyes, hardly opened, wandered, without fixing upon any objects; to our great joy he at length spoke: 'My vision is indistinct,' were his first words. His pulse became more perceptible; his respiration more regular; his sight returned. I then examined the wound to know if there was any dangerous discharge of blood; upon slightly pressing his side it gave him pain; on which I desisted. Soon after recovering his sight, he happened to cast his eye upon the case of pistols, and observing the one that he had had in his hand lying on the outside, he said, 'Take care of that pistol; it is undischarged, and still cocked; it may go off and do harm;—Pendleton knows, (attempting to turn his head towards him) that I did not intend to fire at him.' 'Yes,' said Mr. Pendleton, understanding his wish, 'I have already made Dr. Hosack acquainted with your determination as to that.' He then closed his eyes and remained calm, without any disposition to speak; nor did he say much afterwards, excepting in reply to my questions as to his feelings. He asked me once or twice, how I found his pulse; and he informed me that his lower extremities had lost all feeling; manifesting to me that he entertained no hopes that he should long survive. I changed the posture of his limbs, but to no purpose; they had totally lost their sensibility. Perceiving that we approached the shore, he said, 'Let Mrs. Hamilton be immediately sent for — let the event be gradually broken to her; but give her hopes.' Looking up we saw his friend Mr. Bayard standing on the wharf in great agitation. He had been told by his servant that Gen. Hamilton, Mr. Pendleton, and myself, had crossed the river in a boat together, and too well he conjectured the fatal errand, and foreboded the dreadful result. Perceiving, as we came nearer, that Mr. Pendleton and myself only sat up in the stern sheets, he clasped his hands together in the most violent apprehension; but when I called to him to have a cot prepared, and he at the same moment saw his poor friend lying in the bottom of the boat, he threw up his eyes and burst into a flood of tears and lamentation. Hamilton alone appeared tranquil and composed. We then conveyed him as tenderly as possible up to the house. The distresses of this amiable family were such that till the first shock was abated, they were scarcely able to summon fortitude enough to yield sufficient assistance to their dying friend.

"Upon our reaching the house he became more languid, occasioned probably by the agitation of his removal from the boat. I gave him a little weak wine and water. When he recovered his feelings, he complained of pain in his back; we immediately undressed him, laid him in bed, and darkened the room. I then gave him a large anodyne, which I frequently repeated. During the first day he took upwards of an ounce of laudanum; and tepid anodyne fomentations were also applied to those parts nearest the seat of his pain — Yet were his sufferings, during the whole of the day, almost intolerable.[1] I had not the shadow of a hope of his recovery, and Dr. Post, whom I requested might be sent for immediately on our reaching Mr. Bayard's house, united with me in this opinion. General Rey, the French Consul, also had the goodness to invite the surgeons of the French frigates in our harbour, as they had had much experience in gun-shot wounds, to render their assistance. They immediately came; but to prevent his being disturbed I stated to them his situation, described the nature of his wound and the direction of the ball, with all the symptoms that could enable them to form an opinion as to the event. One of the gentlemen then accompanied me to the bed-side. The result was a confirmation of the opinion that had already been expressed by Dr. Post and myself.

"DURING the night, he had some imperfect sleep; but the succeeding morning his symptoms were aggravated, attended however with a diminution of pain. His mind retained all its usual strength and composure. The great source of his anxiety seemed to be in his sympathy with his half distracted wife and children. He spoke to me frequently of them — 'My beloved wife and children,' were always his expressions. But his fortitude triumphed over his situation, dreadful as it was; once, indeed, at the sight of his children brought to the bed-side together, seven in number, his utterance forsook him; he opened his eyes, gave them one look, and closed them again, till they were taken away. As a proof of his extraordinary

[1] As his habit was delicate and had been lately rendered more feeble by ill health, particularly by a disorder of the stomach and bowels, I carefully avoided all those remedies which are usually indicated on such occasions.

composure of mind, let me add, that he alone could calm the frantic grief of their mother. '*Remember, my Eliza, you are a Christian,*' were the expressions with which he frequently, with a firm voice, but in a pathetic and impressive manner, addressed her. His words, and the tone in which they were uttered, will never be effaced from my memory. At about two o'clock, as the public well knows, he expired.

> " Incorrupta fides — nudaque veritas
> Quando ullum invenient parem?
> Multis ille quidem flebilis occidit.

" I am, Sir,
   " Your friend and humble serv't,
       " DAVID HOSACK.

Wm. Coleman, Esq."

After his death, a note which had been written the evening before the interview, was found addressed to the gentleman who accompanied him to the field; thanking him with tenderness for his friendship to him, and informing him where would be found the keys of certain drawers in his desk, in which he had deposited such papers as he had thought proper to leave behind him; together with his last Will.

The following paper, as containing his motives for accepting the challenge; his reflections on his situation; and some remarks on the conduct of the man, who was to be the cause of his death, is presented as a highly interesting document.

No. XII.

On my expected interview with Col. Burr, I think it proper to make some remarks explanatory of my conduct, motives, and views.

I was certainly desirous of avoiding this interview for the most cogent reasons.

1. My religious and moral principles are strongly opposed to the practice of duelling, and it would ever give me pain to be obliged to shed the blood of a fellow creature in a private combat forbidden by the laws.

2. My wife and children are extremely dear to me, and my life is of the utmost importance to them, in various views.

3. I feel a sense of obligation towards my creditors; who in case of accident to me, by the forced sale of my property, may be in some degree sufferers. I did not think myself at liberty as a man of probity, lightly to expose them to this hazard.

4. I am conscious of no *ill will* to Col. Burr, distinct from political opposition, which, as I trust, has proceeded from pure and upright motives.

Lastly, I shall hazard much, and can possibly gain nothing by the issue of the interview.

But it was, as I conceive, impossible for me to avoid it. There were *intrinsic* difficulties in the thing, and *artificial* embarrassments, from the manner of proceeding on the part of Col. Burr.

INTRINSIC, because it is not to be denied, that my animadversions on the political principles, character, and views of Col. Burr, have been extremely severe; and on different occasions, I, in common with many others, have made very unfavourable criticisms on particular instances of the private conduct of this gentleman.

IN proportion as these impressions were entertained with sincerity, and uttered with motives and for purposes which might appear to me commendable, would be the difficulty (until they could be removed by evidence of their being erroneous,) of explanation or apology. The disavowal required of me by Col. Burr, in a general and indefinite form, was out of my power, if it had really been proper for me to submit to be so questioned; but I was sincerely of opinion that this could not be, and in this opinion, I was confirmed by that of a very moderate and judicious friend whom I consulted. Besides that, Col. Burr appeared to me to assume, in the first instance, a tone unnecessarily peremptory and menacing, and in the second, positively offensive. Yet I wished, as far as might be practicable, to leave a door open to accommodation. This, I think, will be inferred from the written communications made by me and by my direction, and would be confirmed by the conversations between Mr. Van Ness and myself, which arose out of the subject.

I AM not sure whether, under all the circumstances, I did not go further in the attempt to accommodate, than a punctilious delicacy will justify. If so, I hope the motives I have stated will excuse me.

IT is not my design, by what I have said, to affix any odium on the conduct of Col. Burr, in this case. He doubtless has heard of animadversions of mine which bore very hard upon him; and it is probable that as usual they were accompanied with some falsehoods. He may have supposed himself under a necessity of acting as he has done. I hope the grounds of his proceeding have been such as ought to satisfy his own conscience.

I TRUST, at the same time, that the world will do me the justice to believe, that I have not censured him on light grounds, nor from unworthy inducements. I certainly have had strong reasons for what I may have said, though it is possible that in some particulars, I may have been influenced by misconstruction or misinformation. It is also my ardent wish that I may have been more mistaken than I think I have been, and that he, by his future conduct, may show himself worthy of all confidence and esteem, and prove an ornament and blessing to the country.

As well because it is possible that I may have injured Col. Burr, however convinced myself that my opinions and declarations have been well founded, as from my general principles and temper in relation to similar affairs, I have resolved, if our interview is conducted in the usual manner, and it pleases God to give me the opportunity, to *reserve* and *throw away* my first fire, and I *have thoughts* even of *reserving* my second fire — and thus giving a double opportunity to Col. Burr to pause and to reflect.

IT is not, however, my intention to enter into any explanations on the ground — Apology from principle, I hope, rather than pride, is out of the question.

To those who, with me, abhorring the practice of duelling, may think that I ought on no account to have added to the number of bad examples, I answer, that my *relative* situation, as well in public as private, enforcing all the considerations which constitute what men of the world denominate honour, imposed on me (as I thought) a peculiar necessity not to decline the call. The ability to be in future useful, whether in resisting mischief or effecting good, in those crises of our public affairs which seem likely to happen, would probably be inseparable from a conformity with public prejudice in this particular.

A. H.

It is impossible for me to add any thing, that I think will assist the reader in forming a judgment on this affecting paper, written under the solemn impression that it was to be the last he should ever write. I should do an injustice to his memory to say one word, by way of attempting to gain an implicit credit for every syllable it contains. To the head and heart of every reader, then, it is left without comment.

GENERAL HAMILTON'S WILL.

In the name of God, Amen. I, ALEXANDER HAMILTON, of the city of New-York, Counsellor at Law, do make this my last Will and Testament as follows:

First. I appoint John B. Church, Nicholas Fish, and Nathaniel Pendleton, of the city aforesaid, Esquires, to be Executors and Trustees of this my Will;

and I devise to them, their heirs and assigns, as joint tenants and not as tenants in common, all my estate real and personal whatsoever, and wheresoever, upon trust at their discretion, to sell and dispose of the same, at such time and times, in such manner, and upon such terms, as they, the survivors and survivor, shall think fit; and out of the proceeds to pay all the debts which I shall owe at the time of my decease; in whole, if the fund be sufficient; proportionably, if it shall be insufficient; and the residue, if any there shall be, to pay and deliver to my excellent and dear wife Elizabeth Hamilton.

THOUGH, if it should please God to spare my life, I may look for a considerable surplus out of my present property; yet, if he should speedily call me to the eternal world, a forced sale, as is usual, may possibly render it insufficient to satisfy my debts. I pray God that something may remain for the maintenance and education of my dear wife and children. But should it on the contrary happen, that there is not enough for the payment of my debts, I entreat my dear children, if they, or any of them, should ever be able, to make up the deficiency. I, without hesitation, commit to their delicacy a wish which is dictated by my own. — Though conscious that I have too far sacrificed the interests of my family to public avocations, and on this account have the less claim to burthen my children, yet I trust in their magnanimity to appreciate as they ought, this my request. In so unfavourable an event of things, the support of their dear mother, with the most respectful and tender attention, is a duty, all the sacredness of which they will feel. Probably her own patrimonial resources will preserve her from indigence. But in all situations they are charged to bear in mind, that she has been to them the most devoted and best of mothers.

IN testimony whereof I have hereunto subscribed my hand, the ninth day of July, in the year of our Lord one thousand eight hundred and four.

ALEXANDER HAMILTON.

SIGNED, Sealed, Published, and declared, as and for his last Will and Testament, in our presence, who have subscribed the same in his presence, the words *John B. Church* being above interlined.

DOMINIC F. BLAKE,
GRAHAM NEWELL,
THEO. B. VALLEAU.

New-York, Surrogate's Office, ss. — *July* 16*th*, 1804.

I DO hereby certify the preceding to be a true copy of the original Will of Alexander Hamilton, deceased, now on file at my office.

SYLVANUS MILLER, Surrogate.

THE impression which his death made on all classes of people in the city, will best be seen by the following proceedings.

"AT a numerous and respectable meeting of Merchants and other citizens of New-York, at the Tontine Coffee-House, last Evening, Mr. Wm. W. Wolsey was called to the chair, and Mr. Maturin Livingston appointed Secretary.

The Meeting having been informed of the melancholy event of General ALEXANDER HAMILTON's decease, and being deeply sensible of the irreparable loss which the United States have sustained by the death of a man, whose public and private virtues have endeared him to his friends and acquaintances; whose patriotism, talents, integrity, and eminent services, have rendered him peculiarly valuable to his country; and being anxiously desirous to render to so great and distinguished a character the last tribute of respect in their power:

Resolve, That this meeting will unite with their fellow-citizens of all classes in every suitable demonstration of sorrow for the death of General Alexander Hamilton — And that, for this purpose, they recommend to the citizens at large, to shut up their stores, and generally to suspend business on Saturday the 14th inst. and to assemble at the house of Mr. Church, in Robinson-street, at ten o'clock in the forenoon, to form a procession to attend the remains of the deceased:

THAT it be recommended to the owners and masters of vessels to direct the colours of all the vessels in the harbour to be hoisted half mast, during the whole of Saturday next:

THAT Mr. Henderson, Mr. M. Livingston, Mr. A. Jackson, Mr. J. Kane, and Mr. H. I. Wyckoff, be a committee on the part of this meeting, to meet such persons as may be appointed by other bodies of their fellow-citizens, in order to make such further arrangements as the occasion may require.

WILLIAM W. WOOLSEY, Chairman.
MATURIN LIVINGSTON, Secretary.

The Committee of arrangement appointed at the meeting at the Tontine Coffee House on the 12th inst. in conformity with the sense of the meeting, expressed on that occasion, request their fellow-citizens in general to wear Crape on the left arm for thirty days, as a testimony of their respect for the Integrity, Virtues, Talents, and Patriotism, of Gen. ALEXANDER HAMILTON, deceased."

July 13.

" *City of New-York, ss.*

" IN COMMON COUNCIL, July 13, 1804.

"*Resolved unanimously*, That the Common Council of the City of New-York entertain the most unfeigned sorrow and regret for the death of their fellow citizen, ALEXANDER HAMILTON; and with a view to pay a suitable respect to his past life and future memory, and to afford the most unequivocal testimony of the great loss which, in the opinion of the Common Council, not only this city but the state of New-York and the United States have sustained by the death of this great and good man, the Common Council do unanimously recommend that the usual business of the day be dispensed with by all classes of inhabitants:

AND, *Resolved unanimously*, That the ordinance prohibiting the tolling of Bells at funerals be on this occasion suspended, and that it be recommended to those who have the charge of the Church Bells in this City, to cause them to be muffled and tolled at proper intervals during the day of his interment:

AND also, *Resolved unanimously*, That the members of the Common Council will in a body attend and join in the funeral procession of the deceased, at the time and place appointed:

LIKEWISE, *Resolved unanimously*, That a Committee of three be appointed to make such arrangements in behalf and at the expense of the Common Council of the City of New-York, for performing the funeral obsequies of the deceased, as the said Committee shall judge necessary and expedient.

Extract from the Minutes,
T. WORTMAN, Clerk."

" AGREEABLE to notice, the gentlemen of the Bar met at Lovett's Hotel, to join in those expressions of sorrow so universally produced by the untimely death of General Hamilton. The meeting was very numerous, and all party distinction was lost in the general sentiment of love and respect for the illustrious deceased. Mr. Harison, in a few words, with a faltering tongue and a feeling heart, adverted to the sad occasion on which they were called together, and in the most affectionate terms mentioned the private virtues, the splendid talents, and the useful services of this best and greatest of men. Amidst countenances which spoke no common grief the following resolutions were adopted:

" AT a general meeting of the Gentlemen of the Bar of the City of New-York, at Lovett's Hotel, on the 13th of July, 1804; RICHARD HARISON, Esq. in the chair:

This meeting being deeply affected by the death of ALEXANDER HAMILTON, the brightest ornament of their profession, whom they have ever held in the most sincere esteem, and admiration; whose superior talents, distinguished patriotism, eminent services, and uniform integrity, had procured him universal confidence and veneration, and whose loss they lament as a severe private affliction and deplore as a great public calamity:

RESOLVED, that they will unite with their fellow-citizens to demonstrate in every suitable manner their sincere respect for the memory of General HAMILTON, and the deep sense of the loss which their country has sustained.

THAT they will wear crape as mourning for their deceased brother for the space of six weeks.

THAT Jacob Radcliff, Josiah O. Hoffman, Nathan Sanford, John Wells, and Daniel D. Tompkins, be a committee to make any further arrangements that may be proper on this mournful occasion.

DANIEL D. TOMPKINS, Sec'ry."

New-York, 12th July, 1804.

"BRIGADE ORDERS.

" FOR the purpose of paying the last testimony of military respect to Major General ALEXANDER HAMILTON, deceased, the Brigade Company of Artillery, the Sixth Regiment, and the Uniform Companies belonging to the other Regiments of the Brigade, will assemble on Saturday at 9 o'clock, A. M. with three rounds of blank cartridges, in the Park, where they will be joined by the Regiment of Artillery— the whole will be under the command of Lieut. Col. Morton.

By order of Brig. Gen. Boyd,
NATHAN SANFORD,
Assistant Brigade Major."

" P. S. THE Officers not on duty are requested to attend at Mechanic-Hall in uniform, and with the usual mourning."

ARTILLERY.
"REGIMENTAL ORDERS.

" AGREEABLY to Brigade Orders of this date, the First Regiment of Artillery will parade in the Park, on Saturday morning at 9 o'clock. The first battalion with small arms, the second with field artillery: each man of the first battalion will provide himself with three rounds of blank cartridges, to perform the last military obsequies over the grave of the late General HAMILTON.

" CAPTAIN MACLEAN will take charge of firing the minute guns. The officers will appear with crape on the left arm.

By order of Lieut. Col. Curtenius,
ROBERT SWARTWOUT, Adj."

July 12.

" ARTILLERY.

" CAPTAIN DEPEYSTER'S Company will assemble on the Company Parade, at half past 9 o'clock on Saturday morning, in full uniform — Crape to be worn on the left arm.

By order, &c.
J. D. KEESE, Ord. Serjt."

July 13.

"NEW-YORK INDEPENDENT VOLUN-TEERS.

"In pursuance of Regimental Orders of last night, you are ordered to parade on the Battery to-morrow morning, at 9 o'clock precisely, with three rounds of blank cartridges.

By order,
AND. SMITH, Sec."

"A meeting of the *Students at Law* of this City, is requested this evening at 7 o'clock, at the office of Jos. Ogden Hoffman, Esq. in order to consider in what manner they can best express their sincere regret for the death of the late Gen. HAMILTON."

July 13.

"The Students of Columbia College are requested to meet in the College Green to-morrow morning at half after 9 o'clock precisely, with their gowns, for the purpose of joining in the funeral procession of the late General HAMILTON.

N. B. The Graduates of the College are also desired to attend."

"TAMMANIAL NOTICE.

" BROTHERS,

" YOUR attendance is earnestly requested at an extra-meeting of the tribes in the great Wigwam, precisely at the setting of the Sun, this evening, to make arrangements for joining our fellow-citizens and soldiers in a procession, in order to pay the last tribute of national respect due to the manes of our departed fellow-citizen and soldier, General ALEXANDER HAMILTON.

By order of the Grand Sachem,
JAMES D. BISSET, Sec'ry.

SEASON of Fruit, in the year of discovery 312, and of the institution 15th."

July 13.

" THOSE Members of the 'General Society of Mechanics and Tradesmen of the City of New-York,' desirous of paying the last tribute of respect to the remains of General HAMILTON, are requested to meet at their New Hall, on Saturday morning the 14th inst. precisely at 9 o'clock."

" ST. ANDREW'S SOCIETY.

" THE Members of the St. Andrew's Society are requested to meet at the Masonic Hall, to-morrow morning, at half past 9 o'clock precisely, in order to join the Funeral Procession of their late much respected and sincerely beloved Brother, Alexander Hamilton, and to testify the grief and regret they feel, in common with their fellow-citizens, at the irreparable loss this community has sustained by his untimely death.

A. GLASS, Sec'ry."

July 13.

" FUNERAL PROCESSION.

" THE Society of the Cincinnati being charged with the direction of the funeral ceremonies of its President General, the following is the order of procession which will take place to-morrow at Ten o'clock, as commemorative of an event of the deepest national regret.

ORDER OF PROCESSION.

1. The Military Corps commanded by Col. Morton.
2. The Society of the Cincinnati.
3. Clergy of all denominations.
4. The Corpse.
5. The General's Horse.
6. Relations of the deceased.
7. Physicians.
8. The Judges of the Supreme Court.
9. Mr. Gouverneur Morris in his carriage.
10. Gentlemen of the Bar and students at Law.
11. The Governor and Lieutenant Governor of the State.
12. The Mayor and Corporation of the City.
13. Members of Congress and Civil Officers of the United States.
14. The Ministers, Consuls and Residents of Foreign Powers.
15. The Officers of the Army and Navy of the United States.
16. Military and Naval Officers of Foreign Powers.

17. Militia Officers of the State.

18. President, Directors, and Officers of the respective Banks.

19. Chamber of Commerce and Merchants.

20. Marine Society, Wardens of the Port, and Masters and Officers of all vessels in the Harbour.

21. The President, Professors, and Students of Columbia College.

22. The different Societies in such order as their respective Presidents may arrange.

23. The Citizens in general.

THE Military Corps commanded by Col. Morton being ordered to parade in the Park at 10 o'clock, accompanied with Six pieces of Artillery, two of the pieces will remain on the ground under the command of Capt. Maclean, and will fire minute guns from the movement of the Corpse until it arrives at Trinity Church.

THE Sixth Regiment with the Colours and Music of the several Corps, will parade in Robinson street, on the south side fronting Mr. Church's house; Standards and Music in front of the centre—the Regiment in solemn attitude, resting on arms reversed. On waving the Standard of the Cincinnati shrouded in Crape, the Regiment will shoulder and receive the Corpse proceeding from the house with presented arms, the colours and music saluting. On a signal Trumpet the Regiment will shoulder, and the Troops in the Park will throw themselves in columns and occupy the Broadway, with the rear of the column covering the head of Robinson street, and halt. On a signal Trumpet the 6th Regiment in Robinson street will wheel to the right, by Platoons, and occupy the street in front of the Corpse in open

Column, at half distances of Platoons, and with arms reversed wait the signal. On a signal Trumpet the Column will move with Colours and Music in the centre of the 6th Regiment playing the Dead March, with muffled drums. Two companies detached from the military in the Park will cover the flanks of the Corpse, in single file, with trailed arms, from the rear of the 6th Regiment down the line, and take their proper position as the Corpse enters Broadway; the Column advancing will wheel to the left round the Park, enter Beekman-street, and passing down Pearl, will proceed to Whitehall-street, and up Broadway to Trinity Church; the leading wing will form a close column to the right on the Church walk, extending to the north corner of Wall-street, dressing by the left, and facing to the right, stand with ordered arms. The rear wing advancing, will form close column to the left, and facing to the right, extending to the south corner of Wall-street, dressing by the right with ordered arms. Mr. Gouverneur Morris, from the Portico of the Church, (the Corpse in front on a bier) will deliver an appropriate address; at the conclusion of which the Corpse, preceded by the Military and properly attended, will proceed to the Vault, where the military ceremonies will be performed, under the order of the Commandant, which will close the solemnities of the day.

W. S. SMITH, *President.*

W. POPHAM, *Secretary.*"

FUNERAL OBSEQUIES.

On Saturday, the next day, the remains of ALEXANDER HAMILTON were committed to the grave, with every possible testimony of respect and sorrow. The following will present the reader with a correct account of the manner in which the sad solemnities were conducted.

The Military, under the command of Lieutenant Col. Morton, were drawn up in front of Mr. Church's house, in Robinson-street, where the body had been deposited. On the appearance of the corpse it was received by the whole line with presented arms, and saluted by the officers; — melancholy music by a large and elegant Band.

The military then preceded the bier, in open column and inverted order, the left in front, with arms reversed, the band playing a dead march. At 12 o'clock the procession moved in the following order, through Beekman, Pearl, and Whitehall-streets, and up Broadway to the Church :

The Artillery.
The 6th Regiment of Militia.
Flank Companies.
Cincinnati Society.
A numerous train of Clergy of all denominations.

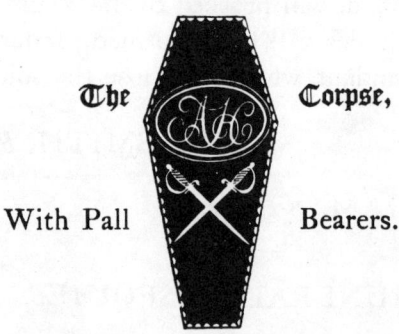

The General's horse appropriately dressed.
His Children and Relatives.

Physicians.
Gouverneur Morris, the funeral orator, in his carriage.
The Gentlemen of the Bar, all in deep mourning.
The Lieutenant-Governor of the State, in his carriage.
Corporation of the city of New-York.
Resident Agents of Foreign Powers.
Officers of our Army and Navy.
Military and Naval Officers of Foreign Powers.
Militia Officers of the State.
The various officers of the respective Banks.
Chamber of Commerce and Merchants.
Wardens of the Port, and masters of vessels in the harbour.
The President, Professors, and Students of Columbia College, in mourning gowns.
St. Andrew's Society, mostly in mourning.
Tammany Society.
Mechanic Society.
Marine Society.
Citizens in general.

The Pall was supported by
General Matthew Clarkson,
Oliver Wolcott, Esquire,
Richard Harison, Esquire,
Abijah Hammond, Esquire,
Josiah Ogden Hoffman, Esquire,
Richard Varick, Esquire,
William Bayard, Esquire, and
His Hon. Judge Lawrence.

ON the top of the coffin was the General's hat and sword; his boots and spurs reversed across the horse. His grey horse, dressed in mourning, was led by two black servants dressed in white, and white turbans trimmed with black.

The streets were lined with people; doors and windows were filled, principally with weeping females, and even the house tops were covered with spectators, who came from all parts to behold the melancholy procession.

When the advanced platoon of the military reached the church, the whole column wheeled backward by sections from the flanks of platoons, forming a lane, bringing their muskets to a reversed order, and resting the cheek on the butt of the piece in the customary attitude of grief. Through the avenue thus formed, the corpse, preceded by the clergy of different denominations and Society of Cincinnati, and followed by the relations of the deceased, and different public bodies, advanced to the church, the band, with drums muffled, playing all the time a pensive, solemn air.

FUNERAL ORATION.

On a stage erected in the portico of Trinity Church, Mr. Gouverneur Morris, having four of General Hamilton's sons, the eldest about sixteen and the youngest about six years of age, with him, rose and delivered to the immense concourse in front an extemporary Oration, which, being pronounced slowly and impressively, was easily committed to memory, and being very soon afterwards placed on paper, is presumed to be correct even to the language.

Fellow-Citizens,

If on this sad, this solemn occasion, I should endeavour to move your commiseration, it would be doing injustice to that sensibility which has been so generally and so justly manifested. Far from attempting to excite your emotions, I must try to repress my own, and yet I fear that instead of the language of a public speaker, you will hear only the lamentations of a bewailing friend. But I will struggle with my bursting heart, to pourtray that Heroic Spirit, which has flown to the mansions of bliss.

STUDENTS of Columbia — he was in the ardent pursuit of knowledge in your academic shades, when the first sound of the American war called him to the field — A young and unprotected volunteer, such was his zeal and so brilliant his service, that we heard his name before we knew his person. — It seemed as if God had called him suddenly into existence, that he might assist to save a world.

THE penetrating eye of Washington soon perceived the manly spirit which animated his youthful bosom. By that excellent judge of men he was selected as an Aid, and thus he became early acquainted with, and was a principal actor in, the most important scenes of our Revolution.

AT the siege of York, he pertinaciously insisted, and he obtained the command of a Forlorn Hope. He stormed the redoubt; but let it be recorded, that not one single man of the enemy perished. His gallant troops, emulating the heroism of their chief, checked the uplifted arm, and spared a foe no longer resisting. Here closed his military career.

SHORTLY after the war, your favour — no, your discernment, called him to public office. You sent him to the convention at Philadelphia: he there assisted in forming that constitution which is now the bond of our union, the shield of our defence, and the source of our prosperity. In signing that compact he exprest his apprehension that it did not contain sufficient means of strength for its own preservation; and that in consequence we should share the fate of many other republics, and pass through Anarchy to Despotism. We hoped better things. We confided in the good sense of the American people; and above all we trusted in the protecting Providence of the Almighty. On this important subject he never concealed his opinion. He disdained concealment. Knowing the purity of his heart, he bore it as it were in his hand, exposing to every passenger its inmost recesses. This generous indiscretion subjected him to censure from misrepresentation. His speculative opinions were treated as deliberate designs; and yet you all know how strenuous, how unremitting were his efforts to establish and to preserve the constitution. If then his opinion was wrong, pardon, oh! pardon that single error, in a life devoted to your service.

At the time when our government was organized, we were without funds, though not without resources. To call them into action, and establish order in the finances, Washington sought for splendid talents, for extensive information, and, above all, he sought for sterling, incorruptible integrity — All these he found in Hamilton. — The system then adopted has been the subject of much animadversion. If it be not without a fault, let it be remembered that nothing human is perfect — Recollect the circumstances of the moment — recollect the conflict of opinion — and above all, remember that *the minister of a republic must bend to the will of the people.* The administration which Washington formed, was one of the best that any country was ever blest with. And the result was a rapid advance in power and prosperity, of which there is no example in any other age or nation. The part which Hamilton bore is universally known.

His unsuspecting confidence in professions which he believed to be sincere, led him to trust too much to the undeserving. This exposed him to misrepresentation. He felt himself obliged to resign — The care of a rising family, and the narrowness of his fortune, made it a duty to return to his profession for their support. But though he was compelled to abandon public life, never, no, never for a moment did he abandon the public service. He never lost sight of your interests——I declare to you, before that God in whose presence we are now so especially assembled, that in his most private and confidential conversations, the single objects of discussion and consideration were your freedom and happiness.

You well remember the state of things which again called forth Washington from his retreat to lead your armies. You know that he asked for Hamilton to be his second in command. That venerable sage well knew the dangerous incidents of a military profession, and he felt the hand of time pinching life at its source. It was probable that he would soon be removed from the scene, and that his second would succeed to the command. He knew, by experience, the importance of that place —- and he thought the sword of America might safely be confided to the hand which now lies cold in that coffin. Oh! my fellow-citizens, remember this solemn testimonial, that he was not ambitious. Yet he was charged with ambition; and wounded by the imputation. when he laid down his command, he declared, in the proud independence of his soul, that he never would accept of any office, unless in a foreign war he should be called on to expose his life in defence of his country. This determination was immovable. It was his fault that his opinions and his resolutions could not be changed. Knowing his own firm purpose, he was indignant at the charge that he sought for place or power. He was ambitious only of glory, but he was deeply solicitous for you. For himself he feared nothing, but he feared that bad men might, by false professions, acquire your confidence, and abuse it to your ruin.

BRETHREN of the Cincinnati — There lies our chief! Let him still be our model. Like him, after long and faithful public service, let us cheerfully perform the social duties of private life. Oh! he was mild and gentle. In him there was no offence; no guile — his generous hand and heart were open to all.

GENTLEMEN of the Bar — You have lost your brightest ornament. Cherish and imitate his example. While, like him, with justifiable, with laudable zeal, you pursue the interests of your clients, remember, like him, the eternal principles of justice.

FELLOW-CITIZENS — You have long witnessed his professional conduct, and felt his unrivalled eloquence. You know how well he performed the duties of a Citizen — you know that he never courted your favour by adulation, or the sacrifice of his own judgment. You have seen him contending against you, and saving your dearest interests, as it were, in spite of yourselves. And you now feel and enjoy the benefits resulting from the firm energy of his conduct. Bear this testimony to the memory of my departed friend. I CHARGE YOU TO PROTECT HIS FAME — It is all he has left — all that these poor orphan children will inherit from their father. But, my countrymen, that Fame may be a rich treasure to you also. Let it be the test by which to examine those who solicit your favour. Disregarding professions, view their conduct, and on a doubtful occasion, ask, *Would Hamilton have done this thing?*

You all know how he perished. On this last scene, I cannot, I must not dwell. It might excite emotions too strong for your better judgment. Suffer not your indignation to lead to any act which might again offend the insulted majesty of the law; on his part, as from his lips, though with my voice — for his voice you will hear no more, — let me entreat you to respect yourselves.

AND now, ye ministers of the everlasting God, perform your holy office, and commit these ashes of our departed brother to the bosom of the Grave!

THE oration being finished the corpse was carried to the grave, where the usual funeral service was performed by the Reverend Bishop Moore. The troops who had entered the church-yard, formed an extensive hollow square, and terminated the solemnities with three vollies over the grave.

DURING the procession there was a regular discharge of minute guns from the Battery, by a detachment from the regiment of artillery. The different merchant vessels in the harbour wore their colours half mast, both this and the preceding day.

His Britannic Majesty's ship of war Boston, Capt. Douglass, at anchor within the Hook, appeared in mourning the whole morning, and at 10 o'clock she commenced firing minute guns, which were continued 48 minutes. His Majesty's packet Lord Charles Spencer, Capt. Cotesworth, also was in mourning, and fired an equal number of guns. The French frigates Cybelle and Didon, were also put into full mourning both this and the preceding day, with yards peeked; they also fired minute guns during the procession. These marks of attention will be gratefully received by our fellow-citizens, as evidence how highly the deceased was respected and esteemed by the French and English officers.

END OF PART I.

A COLLECTION, &c.

N°. II.

THE following extracts from the several daily papers, will serve to show the strong impression which the death of General Hamilton made on the hearts of his fellow-citizens; those who knew him best.

THE EVENING POST.

WITH emotions that we have not the hand to inscribe, have we to announce the death of ALEXANDER HAMILTON. He was cut off in the 48th year of his age, in the full vigour of his faculties, and in the midst of all his usefulness.

WE have not the firmness to depict this melancholy, heartrending event. Now—when death has extinguished all party animosity, the gloom that over-spreads every countenance, the sympathy that pervades every bosom, bear irresistible testimony of the esteem and respect all maintained for him; of the love all bore him; and assure us that an impression has been made by his loss which no time can efface. It becomes us not to enter into particulars; we have no doubt, that, in compliance with the universal anxiety of our citizens, a statement will soon be exhibited to them containing all the circumstances necessary to enable them to form a just opinion of this tragic scene. In the mean time we offer the following letter that we have received from the Reverend Bishop Moore. The testimony which this pious and venerable Clergyman bears to the virtues of the deceased, will, we are sure, not be lost on a discerning community.

TO THE EDITOR OF THE EVENING POST.

Thursday Evening, July 12.

MR. COLEMAN,

THE public mind being extremely agitated by the melancholy fate of that great man, ALEXANDER HAMILTON, I have thought it would be grateful to my fellow-citizens, would provide against misrepresentation, and, perhaps, be conducive to the advancement of the cause of religion, were I to give a narrative of some facts which have fallen under my own observation, during the time which elapsed between the fatal duel and his departure out of this world.

YESTERDAY morning, immediately after he was brought from Hoboken to the house of Mr. Bayard, at Greenwich, a message was sent informing me of the sad event, accompanied by a request from General Hamilton, that I would come to him for the purpose of administering the Holy Communion. I went; but being desirous to afford time for serious reflection, and conceiving that under existing circumstances, it would be right and proper to avoid every appearance of precipitancy in performing one of the most solemn offices of our religion, I did not then comply with his desire. At one o'clock I was again called on to visit him. Upon my entering the room and approaching his bed, with the utmost calmness and composure he said, " My dear Sir, you perceive my unfortunate situation, and no doubt have been made acquainted with the circumstances which led to it. It is my desire to receive the Communion at your hands. I hope you will not conceive there is any impropriety in my request." He added, " It has for some time past been the wish of my heart, and it was my intention to take an early opportunity of uniting myself to the church, by the reception of that holy ordinance." I observed to him, that he must be very sensible of the delicate and trying situation in which I was then placed; that however desirous I might be to afford consolation to a fellow mortal in distress; still, it was my duty as a minister of the gospel, to hold up the law of God as paramount to all other law; and that, therefore, under the influence of such sentiments, I must unequivocally condemn the practice which had brought him to his present unhappy condition. He acknowledged the propriety of these sentiments, and declared that he viewed the late transaction with sorrow and contrition. I then asked him, " Should it please God, to restore you to health, Sir, will you never be again engaged in a similar transaction? and will you employ all your influence in society to discountenance this barbarous custom?" His answer was, " That, Sir, is my deliberate intention."

I PROCEEDED to converse with him on the subject of his receiving the Communion; and told him that with respect to the qualifications of those who wished to become partakers of that holy ordinance, my inquiries could not be made in language more expressive than that which was used by our Church. — " Do you sincerely repent of your sins past? Have you a lively faith in God's mercy through Christ, with a thankful remembrance of the death of Christ? And are you disposed to live in love and charity with all men?" He lifted up his hands and said, " With the utmost sincerity of heart I can answer those questions in the affirmative — I have no ill will against Col. Burr. I met him with a fixed resolution to do him no harm — I forgive all that happened." I then observed to him, that the terrors of the divine law were to be announced to the obdurate and impenitent: but that the consolations of the Gospel were to be offered to the humble and contrite heart: that I had no reason to doubt his sincerity, and would proceed immediately to gratify his wishes. The Communion was then administered, which he received with great devotion, and his heart afterwards appeared to be perfectly at rest. I saw him again this morning, when, with his last faultering words, he expressed a strong confidence in the mercy of God through the intercession of the Redeemer. I remained with him until 2 o'clock this afternoon, when death closed the awful scene — he expired without a struggle, and almost without a groan.

By reflecting on this melancholy event, let the humble believer be encouraged ever to hold fast that precious faith which is the only source of true consolation in the last extremity of nature. Let the infidel be persuaded to abandon his opposition to that gospel which the strong, inquisitive, and comprehensive mind of a HAMILTON embraced, in his last moments, as the truth from heaven. Let those who are disposed to justify the practice of duelling, be induced, by this simple narrative, to view with abhorrence that custom which has occasioned an irreparable loss to a worthy and most afflicted family; which has deprived his friends of a beloved companion, his profession of one of its brightest ornaments, and his country of a great statesman and a real patriot.

With great respect,
I remain your friend and servant,
BENJAMIN MOORE.

Though not in chronological order, yet here may be the most proper place for the Rev'd Dr. Mason's letter, as it relates to the same subject.

TO THE EDITOR OF THE EVENING POST.

Sir,

Having read, in the Commercial Advertiser of the 16th, a very imperfect account of my conversation with General Hamilton, the day previous to his decease, I judge it my duty to lay the following narrative before the public.

On the morning of Wednesday, the 11th inst. shortly after the rumour of the General's injury had created an alarm in the city, a note from Dr. Post informed me that " he was extremely ill at Mr. Wm. Bayard's, and expressed a particular desire to see me as soon as possible." I went immediately.* The exchange of melancholy salutation, on entering the General's apartment, was succeeded by a silence which he broke by saying, that he " had been anxious to see me, and have the sacrament administered to him; and that this was still his wish." I replied, that " it gave me unutterable pain to receive from him any request to which I could not accede: that, in the present instance, a compliance was incompatible with all my obligations; as it is a principle in our

* Perhaps it may not be amiss, in order that no misapprehension should be created by the letters themselves, which are not very explicit on that point, that Bishop Moore was first sent for, but left the house without complying at that time with Gen. Hamilton's wish ; that Dr. Mason was then sent for, who, as he says in his letter, told him he could not accede to his request ; that the Bishop was sent for a second time, who came and administered the sacrament, as related by himself. This explanatory note is added because a misapprehension of facts, gave rise at the time to some small altercation between anonymous writers in one of our daily prints.

churches never to administer the Lord's Supper privately to any person under any circumstances." He urged me no further. I then remarked to him, that " the Holy Communion is an exhibition and pledge of the mercies which the Son of God has purchased; that the absence of the sign does not exclude from the mercies signified; which were accessible to him by faith in their gracious author." "I am aware," said he, " of that. It is only as a sign that I wanted it." A short pause ensued. I resumed the discourse, by observing that " I had nothing to address to him in his affliction, but that same *gospel of the grace of God*, which it is my office to preach to the most obscure and illiterate : that in the sight of God all men are on a level, as *all have sinned, and come short of his glory;* and that they must apply to him for pardon and life, *as sinners,* whose only refuge is in his *grace reigning by righteousness through our Lord Jesus Christ.*" "I perceive it to be so," said he; "I am a sinner: I look to his mercy." I then adverted to " the infinite merit of the Redeemer, as the *propitiation for sin*, the sole ground of our acceptance with God ; the sole channel of his favour to us; and cited the following passages of scripture :— *There is no other name given under heaven among men, whereby we must be saved, but the name of Jesus. He is able to save them to the uttermost who come unto God by him, seeing he ever liveth to make intercession for them. The blood of Jesus Christ cleanseth from all sin.*" This last passage introduced the affair of the duel, on which I reminded the General, that he was not to be instructed as to its moral aspect; that *the precious blood of Christ* was as effectual and as necessary to wash away the transgression which had involved him in suffering, as any other transgression ; and that he must there, and there alone, seek peace for his con-

science, and a hope that should "*not make him ashamed.*"
He assented, with strong emotion, to these representations, and declared his abhorrence of the whole transaction. "It was always," added he, "against my principles. I used every expedient to avoid the interview; but I have found, for some time past, that my life *must* be exposed to that man. I went to the field determined not to take *his* life." He repeated his disavowal of all intention to hurt Mr. Burr; the anguish of his mind in recollecting what had passed; and his humble hope of forgiveness from his God. I recurred to the topic of the divine compassion; the freedom of pardon in the Redeemer Jesus to perishing sinners. "That grace, my dear General, which brings salvation, is rich, rich" — "Yes," interrupted he, "it is *rich* grace." "And on that grace," continued I, "a sinner has the highest encouragement to repose his confidence, because it is tendered to him upon the surest foundation; the scripture testifying that *we have redemption through the blood of Jesus, the forgiveness of sins according to the richness of his grace.*" Here the General, letting go my hand, which he had held from the moment I sat down at his bed-side, clasped his hands together, and, looking up towards heaven, said, with emphasis, "I *have* a tender reliance on the mercy of the Almighty, through the merits of the Lord Jesus Christ." He replaced his hand in mine, and appearing somewhat spent, closed his eyes. A little after, he fastened them on me, and I proceeded. "The *simple* truths of the Gospel, my dear Sir, which require no abstruse investigation, but faith in the veracity of God who cannot lie, are best suited to your present condition, and they are full of consolation." "I feel them to be so," replied he. I then repeated these texts of Scripture: — *It is a faithful saying, and worthy of all*

acceptation, that Christ Jesus came into the world to save sinners, and of sinners the chief. I, even I, am he that blotteth out thy transgressions for mine own sake, and will not remember thy sins. Come now, and let us reason together, saith the Lord; though your sins be as scarlet, they shall be white as snow; though they be red like crimson, they shall be as wool. " This," said he, " is my support. Pray for me." " Shall I pray with you?" " Yes." I prayed with him, and heard him whisper as I went along ; which I supposed to be his concurrence with the petitions. At the conclusion he said, " Amen. God grant it."

BEING about to part with him, I told him " I had one request to make." He asked " what it was?" I answered, " that whatever might be the issue of his affliction, he would give his testimony against the practice of duelling." " I will," said he, " I have done it. If *that*," evidently anticipating the event, " if *that* be the issue, you will find it in writing. If it please God that I recover, I shall do it in a manner which will effectually put me out of its reach in future." I mentioned, once more, the importance of renouncing every other dependence for the eternal world, but the mercy of God in Christ Jesus ; with a particular reference to the catastrophe of the morning. The General was affected, and said, " Let us not pursue the subject any further, it agitates me." He laid his hands upon his breast, with symptoms of uneasiness, which indicated an increased difficulty of speaking. I then took my leave. He pressed my hand affectionately, and desired to see me again at a proper interval. As I was retiring, he lifted up his hands in the attitude of prayer, and said feebly, " God be merciful to ———" His voice sunk, so that I heard not the rest distinctly, but understood him to quote the words of the publican in the gospel, and to end the sentence with, " me a sinner."

I saw him, a second time, on the morning of Thursday; but from his appearance, and what I had heard, supposing that he could not speak without severe effort, I had no conversation with him. I prayed for a moment at his bed-side, in company with his overwhelmed family and friends; and for the rest, was one of the mourning spectators of his composure and dignity in suffering. His mind remained in its former state : and he viewed with calmness his approaching dissolution. I left him between twelve and one, and at two, as the public know, he breathed his last.

I am, Sir,
With much respect,
Your obedient servant,
J. M. MASON.

New-York, July 18*th,* 1804.

THE DAILY ADVERTISER.

It is with sentiments of the deepest regret that we announce to the public the decease of the great and estimable General Alexander Hamilton. No event since the death of the illustrious Washington has filled the public mind with more painful solicitude, or so much called forth the general sympathy and grief, as the event we now record. The loss of a character, so much respected in his profession, so esteemed by the public, so beloved in the circles of private friendship and of domestic life, is beyond the power of expression; and the *manner* of his death ! — Alas! it can be remembered only with unmingled horror and regret.

VAIN were the attempt to give even a hasty sketch of the various, the unequalled merit of the illustrious deceased — the task will be executed by an abler hand. Suffice it, under the present impression of public regret, to state —

THAT, as a *soldier*, through the whole of our revolutionary war, General Hamilton was eminently distinguished. He was one of the few select friends of the Commander in Chief, often tried and as often approved. His cool and active valour in storming the redoubt before York-Town will never be forgotten. After such a splendid proof of bravery, was it necessary again to put it to the test in compliance with a false notion of honour?

As a *statesman*, Gen. Hamilton added still greater honour to his name. To him are we principally indebted for the national constitution and the system of laws under which we now live. It was his hand that traced the outlines of our most important municipal institutions. To him we owe the plans for the organization of our National Treasury, the provisions for the payment of the public debt, for the establishment of the banks, of the mint, and the whole revenue system of our country.

As a *lawyer*, he was unrivalled at the bar. His talents and eloquence gave him a decided ascendancy in his profession, which, however, was softened by the most unaffected modesty, and the utmost courtesy and gentleness.

As a *man*, no one was more highly esteemed for his perfect integrity, truth, candour, and public spirit, than the unfortunate deceased. He enjoyed (and no man ever better deserved it) the unlimited confidence of his friends and fellow-citizens.

As a *christian*, we are happy to add, he has not left the world to doubt of his *faith* and *hope*. In his last hours he has put a seal on his character, by declaring his firm belief in the merits and atonement of a SAVIOUR; by avowing his trust in Redeeming grace, and by requesting and receiving in attestation of his faith, the sacrament of the Lord's Supper.

HASTY and imperfect as the foregoing outlines may be, they will recall to the public mind, those impressions of exalted merit which we are sure will never be obliterated, will never cease to be cherished with a melancholy pleasure. The soldier, the statesman, the man of preeminent talents and worth, is gone; but his virtues will be had in memory, will be admired and recorded, wherever there is a heart to feel, or a tongue to repeat the eulogy, due to departed worth.

WITH the deeply afflicted consort, and the orphan children of the deceased general, the public will sincerely sympathize. *Their* loss is incalculable. May heaven support them on this trying occasion. May they enjoy consolations from above (for the world can now have few for *them*); consolations which are neither few nor small, beyond the reach of accident and change.

SAME PAPER.

THE ceremonies of Saturday were conducted according to the published arrangements. The scene was indeed solemn and impressive. Every countenance evinced a sorrow to which only a loss of the first magnitude — an event of the most tragical nature, could give rise. Every mark of respect to which departed worth has a claim, was paid with affectionate earnestness. — Business was universally suspended, and the whole city crowded either to perform or to witness the funeral honours due to the illustrious deceased. About noon, the different bodies forming the procession, having taken their respective places, the corpse was conducted from the house of John B. Church Esq. and the whole began to move. The moment was deeply impressive. Every thing conspired to solemnize the mind. The tolling of the deep-toned bells — the melting melody of the music — the slow and melancholy-inspiring pace of the procession — the appearance of the sable coffin with its accompanyments — the sons of the deceased, still of tender age, clad in the vestments of woe, and shedding the tear of anguish over the fate of a beloved father — (Unhappy youths! who will now be the guide of your growing years, the guardian of your budding virtues?) These, with the awe-striking report of the minute guns, to which every heart beat its sad response, rendered the whole a scene of solemn woe. Two hours elapsed before the procession reached the place of interment, owing to the slowness of the pace and length of the rout. Arrived at Trinity Church, the Hon. Gouverneur Morris ascended a stage prepared for him, and delivered to a deeply-impressed audience, an appropriate and pathetic address. He sketched the life, the talents, the virtues, the civil and military services of the deceased. He addressed himself particularly to the students of Columbia College, the gentlemen of the bar, the Cincinnati Society, and the military. He adverted to the deplorable cause of the disaster, by stating that all were acquainted with it, and that he could not then say a word on the sad subject. The orator having concluded, the body was then interred with the accustomed military honours. Thus has perished, by an untimely death, a patriot of exalted merit, a soldier and a civilian of pre-eminent worth. Thus has America been bereft of her second Washington!

THE NEW-YORK GAZETTE.

LAST Saturday were interred, with all possible respect, the remains of Gen. ALEXANDER HAMILTON, the enlightened statesman, the skilful lawyer, the eloquent orator, the disinterested patriot, and the honest man. Never was the sensibility of the citizens awakened to such a degree, and never did they witness so mournful a scene. It renewed their grief for the death of Washington, to see his friend and counsellor cut off in the highest vigour of his faculties, and the United States deprived of their great earthly stay.

IMMEDIATELY after his decease, the bells announced that he was no more. On the morning of the day of his funeral, all the bells were muffled, and tolled from six to seven o'clock. They began again at ten, and continued until the procession reached the church. The ships in the harbour exhibited the usual tokens of mourning, and minute guns were fired from the forts, and from American and foreign armed vessels. The bells again tolled from seven to eight in the evening.

THE procession, consisting of the military, the Cincinnati, the clergy of all denominations, the gentlemen of the bar and students at law, strangers, the different incorporate bodies, the several societies, together with the citizens, was very large. All vied with one another in testifying their sense of the worth of the illustrious man deceased, and the irreparable loss which the country had sustained. The sides of the streets were crowded, and the windows were filled with spectators, and many climbed up into trees and got on the tops of houses. Not a smile was visible, and hardly a whisper was to be heard, but tears were seen rolling down the cheeks of the affected multitude.

When the front of the procession had advanced as far as Trinity Church, they halted; and an oration was delivered by Gouverneur Morris, from a stage which had been previously erected in the portico of the Church. The notice given to the Orator was so short, his own feelings and those of the audience so great, that he was able only to paint in an imperfect manner the character and services of the first and most beloved citizen. A little time hence, more justice can be done to his transcendent merits; and the future historian will seize them with eagerness to adorn his page.

The General, during his short illness, spoke with the utmost abhorrence of the practice of duelling, and has left his testimony against it. This is known to have been long his sentiment. He declared that he had no ill-will against his antagonist, and had determined to do him no harm; professed his firm belief of the Christian religion, and his " tender reliance on the mercy of Almighty God through the merits of the Lord Jesus Christ;" he devoutly received the holy sacrament, at his own earnest request. The witness of a man of such extensive powers and information, will outweigh that of an host of infidels. This completes his character, and demonstrates that he was good as well as great. "How are the mighty fallen, and the weapons of war perished!" "As a man falleth before wicked men, so fallest thou: And all the people wept again over him."

THE AMERICAN CITIZEN. (*Democratic.*)

General Hamilton's Funeral.* — On Saturday last the remains of this gentleman were interred, accompanied with military honours, in the family vault, Trinity Church-yard.

ALTHOUGH the period which elapsed between his death and his funeral was but short, yet the lively recollection of his Revolutionary services — his acknowledged superior genius — his transcendent talents — his private worth — his sterling integrity, and the amiable frankness of his heart, excited in our citizens an uncommon cordiality and vigour to testify their high sense of these virtues by every demonstration of respect. There was a very general suspension of business, and the streets were uncommonly crowded with spectators.

THE scene was impressive; and what added unspeakably to its solemnity, was the mournful group of tender boys, the sons, the once hopes and joys of the deceased, who, with tears gushing from their eyes, sat upon the stage, at the feet of the orator, bewailing the loss of their

---

* AT present we shall say nothing of the *cause* or *manner* of his death. On these points we have much to lay before the public; but prudence dictates silence until we are furnished with correct information from authentic sources. The public have an indubitable right to be informed of the *cause* and *manner* of his lamented fate. This information is demanded by the feelings of our citizens; by a voice too powerful to be resisted. I trust it will not be long delayed. Every incident of this catastrophe is interesting.

parent! It was too much; the sternest powers, the bloodiest villain, could not resist the melting scene. I wish I could go on and describe the sensations I felt, and those which were manifest on every countenance.

SAME PAPER.

General Hamilton's Death.—The Editor, in all humility, asks the reader to accompany him through a brief review of the correspondence, recently published, in relation to the unhappy affair which terminated the existence of the illustrious deceased. He enters upon this unpleasant task the more readily and with the more zeal, since he views, and cannot but view, the death of General Hamilton as a national loss, and as the inevitable and deplorable effect of a *long meditated and predetermined system of hostility on the part of Mr. Burr and his confidential advisers.*

LEST, however, he may be misunderstood by some, and knowingly and injuriously misrepresented by others, he deems it fit to cause himself to be clearly and distinctly understood. This, perhaps, is an homage due to the *honest* errors of the less liberal part of the community.

To a *few* of those with whom I think, and act in whatever relates to the administration of the State, and General Governments, it may seem extraordinary that I, who while the General lived to give comfort to his family, and splendour to his nation, was opposed to him on *some* political points, should, when laid in the cold and silent tomb, become a guardian of his fame, a vindicator of his wrongs. If in the Republican party there is *one man* of this description, (and I trust there is not) I would with diffidence beg him to *reflect*, and to exercise, with becoming dignity and moderation, those intellectual powers which it hath pleased God to impart even to the humblest of his image. I ask only for the privilege of thinking, and of expressing my thoughts with exemption from cruel and overbearing intolerance. A fixed determination, however, to enjoy the one, will prompt me to a due resistance of the other. I must unthink what I have thought, and unlearn what I know, before I can act the part of a *savage;* and he deceives himself who concludes that, in my editorial pursuits, I will be guided by any opinions but my own. With conscious, and, as I think, becoming pride, I utterly disclaim and renounce that illiberality which will not award to illustrious merit its just due. I have, and always had, an exalted opinion of the merits of the deceased, and with unaffected sincerity and deep regret lament his loss.

THIS opinion and this sentiment, however, will not be construed by the liberal and the enlightened, into an approbation of the political maxims of this great statesman, nor into a dereliction of principles formerly maintained, and still tenaciously adhered to. It is the high prerogative, the distinguishing power of the human mind, and most honourable to man, justly to discriminate in whatever relates to the fame of those pre-eminent citizens who give character and lustre to a nation. HAMILTON, I believe, entertained political opinions at variance with mine, and on which, manifested in many instances by the administration of Mr. Adams, and, in *one*, by that of General Washington, I cannot, without unpleasant sensations, reflect. From these, which while living I opposed, I still dissent; but, alas! he is dead, and I cannot pursue him to the grave for *opinions* HONESTLY entertained, calmly and dignifiedly asserted, luminously and instructively enforced, and conveyed to the public with all the elegance of a scholar, and enriched with all the erudition of a distinguished jurist. I leave it to presumptuous arrogance, to a species of party rancour which I disclaim, to take another course.

So far I differed from General Hamilton in political opinion; but all difference is now at an end. Death has *swallowed up* in *victory*, cruel and fatal victory, the narrow isthmus that separated from this great luminary, those with whom I act. I know that ancient writers urge with force and propriety, and that modern politicians acknowledge, as with one accord, the necessity of frequently laying before the people, by way of admonition, and to put them on their guard, the *vices* of great men, even after death has destroyed the power of repetition. But were I asked whether General Hamilton had *vices*; in the face of the world, in the presence of my God, I would answer, NO. Like all men he sometimes *erred*; but I cannot admit, that even his *errors* were those of the *heart*. He was human, and therefore not perfect. But if we correctly judge of human perfection by *purity of heart*, by *rectitude of intention*, I hesitate not to say, that, in my opinion, General Hamilton was most perfect.

His private virtues, his public services, his great abilities, involuntarily excite in me the warmest esteem for his memory.

Of his private virtues there is no difference of opinion. All men of all parties, speak of them with rapture, and acknowledge them with admiration. To these, vice pays voluntary homage. The plotting, mischievous citizen, whose bloody hand, guided by cool malignancy, terminated his existence, will acknowledge them. In all the private relations of life he was honest, faithful, generous, and humane. His heart was the seat of every manly virtue. No man ever impeached his integrity with any colour of justice. In vain have party collisions and rancour ransacked public records, and exhausted private inquisition for a blemish. The fatal catastrophe proves, that, like Aristides, he chose to yield his life, rather than his integrity. SUCH A MAN, *whatever were his political opinions*, irresistibly commands our esteem.

His public services were many, splendid, and great. From these, nothing but deplorable infatuation, nothing but fiery zeal, unmixt with a ray of reflection, can withhold a lasting glow of admiration and gratitude. The friend of liberty, he who for a moment reflects that out of the revolutionary contest, that chaos of clashing elements, arose A WORLD OF FREEDOM, cannot but venerate the memory of those who, as it were, created it. In this most glorious, most useful, most splendid of earthly scenes, HAMILTON performed a conspicuous — shall I not say a disinterested, a patriotic part? Scarcely arrived at the " gristle of manhood ; " glowing with patriotic fire, with military ardour; he joined the creative phalanx, and signalized himself by constancy, by perseverance, by valour; and irradiated, with the rays of his superior genius, all within the sphere of its presence. His revolutionary services entitle him to our affection, and will endear his memory to all who are sincerely attached to our independence.

His civil was more brilliant than his military career.

His early efforts as a statesman, excel in utility and lustre his exertions in the field. Perhaps to him, more than to any other man, we are indebted for the excellent constitution under which we live. Whatever aberrations from republican maxims, rigorous inquisition may have discovered in his efforts in the convention, I *know* not; but this I may predict, from what we *do know*, that his numerous essays, under the title of " FEDERALIST," advocating the principles and enforcing the adoption of the constitution, will immortalize his name, and render him illustrious when every memento of the cavilling witlings of the day shall be swept from the records of time, and buried in everlasting forgetfulness. I think I am not incorrect when I say, that these essays are the *ablest political papers in the world*. They are replete with lessons of wisdom, clothed in unusual elegance. They are the production of a mind naturally capacious and enriched with all the lore of learning. I read them with renewed pleasure and instruction. Amidst the afflictions of the relatives of the deceased, it cannot but be pleasing to witness statesmen and jurists * resorting to this elementary work as an unerring standard by which to test and determine matters in controversy.

THE MERCANTILE ADVERTISER.

THE remains of the late General HAMILTON were on Saturday afternoon deposited in the " house appointed for all living." The mournful procession moved from his friend Mr. Church's in Robinson-street, about eleven o'clock, in the order directed by the Committee of Arrangements; and it was not until near two that the rear reached Trinity Church, so numerous were the citizens who joined in paying this last tribute to the memory of

* See Tucker's Blackstone and Debates in Congress.

the illustrious dead. We never witnessed, in this country or in Europe, on any similar occasion, so general a sorrow, such an universal regret, or a ceremonial more awful and impressive.

T HE arduous task of delivering an Oration over the body of the deceased, was committed to the splendid talents of Mr. Gouverneur Morris; and he executed it in a manner highly honourable to his feelings. He sought not, in the course of it, to inflame those passions in the people which had already risen to no ordinary height, but touched lightly on the circumstance which produced the lamentable event; and dwelt with peculiar felicity on the public and private virtues, the uncommon talents, the great usefulness, the inflexible integrity, and the real patriotism of his departed friend. His discourse was necessarily short, for his sensibility sometimes almost deprived him of the power of utterance.

THE COMMERCIAL ADVERTISER.

T HUS has the last kind office been performed by our bereaved, afflicted city, to the remains of our country's brightest ornament. In the long train of mourners on this melancholy occasion, every countenance was covered with sadness, every heart oppressed with sorrow. Never, but at the loss of our beloved W ASHINGTON, has the voice of mourning been so impressively heard, nor the grief of our citizens so universally and emphatically expressed. Well may our city and our country mourn!— Hamilton, in the prime of life, and the vigour of talents and of usefulness, has been hurried to an untimely grave! He whose unequalled skill, and undaunted courage at the siege of York-Town, gave victory to our arms, and peace to our country — whose transcendent talents, and unwearied efforts, contributed essentially to the erection of our national fabric — who organized our financial system, and established our public credit — who was the favourite counsellor and friend of Washington — who invariably sacrificed private gain, and personal honour at the shrine of public good — whose comprehensive, powerful and intuitive mind formed the boast and glory of America — the illustrious, the eloquent Hamilton, has fallen by the hand of a desperate and relentless foe!

Who would believe, had not the fact evinced it, that the *son* of the venerable President Burr, that model of christian patience, charity, and meekness, whose instruction, and whose example equally tended to impress the utmost kindness and good-will to all men — that the *son* of *such* a man, the second officer in the United States, should, in direct violation of the laws of heaven and of his own state — in violation of the most sacred principles of religion and morality, and after every means of reconciliation on the part of the unfortunate deceased, that was consistent with honour (as we are informed) had been exhausted — should take a cool and deadly aim against the *first citizen* of our country — the father of a numerous family — the husband of a most affectionate wife — an ornament to his country and to human nature? Could nothing but his blood atone for a few hasty expressions, indiscreet as they regarded his personal safety, but honestly intended for the public good, and authorized by every just principle of an elective government? Could nothing allay the cool, persevering resentment of his antagonist, but the heart's blood of such a man?

Well! he is gone! Gone, with the tenderest esteem, the highest respect, the most affectionate tears, that ever fell on the tomb of a public character! He has gone, we trust, to receive the rich reward of his "labours of love" — of the many and great exertions for his country's welfare. Trusting in the merits of his Saviour — penitent for his past sins — forgiving even the foe from whom he received his mortal wound — he is gone amidst the gush of sorrow from the eyes of weeping thousands, to receive that recompense of reward, which is the meed of the truly upright and benevolent.

On this deeply affecting subject much more could be said: but we pause —

" To those who know him not, no words can paint,
" And those who knew him, know all words are faint."

The following will show the impression made by the melancholy event in Philadelphia.

TRIBUTE OF RESPECT.

The Citizens of Philadelphia, Southwark, and the Northern Liberties, assembled agreeably to public notice, for the purpose of adopting proper measures for the expression of their grief at the untimely fate of their deceased fellow-citizen, Major-General ALEXANDER HAMILTON, their admiration of his virtues and his talents — and their gratitude for the eminent services, which as a soldier and statesman, he has rendered to his country —

Resolve, That a National tribute of respect to the memory of departed Heroes and Statesmen, not only excites an emulation of their glorious example, but constitutes the purest reward of their toils and their virtues;

and that such a tribute is justly due to the memory of ALEXANDER HAMILTON.

THAT in imitation of the pious example of the deceased, in the closing scenes of his life, exhibiting an illustrious proof of the benign influence of the religion of our forefathers, the citizens, in their respective places of worship, on Sunday next, will render their prayers of thanksgiving to GOD, for his goodness in having blessed our nation with men of talents to discern, and of virtue to pursue, her safety, her honour, and her welfare; and especially for having, thus long, continued to us the eminently useful talents of the deceased.

THAT the Clergymen of the several denominations be requested to expatiate on the same day upon the irreligious and pernicious tendency of a custom, which has deprived our country of one of her best and most invaluable citizens, and has proved so fatally destructive to the happiness of his family.

THAT arrangements be made for having the bells throughout the city muffled and tolled during the day, and that the Merchants will direct the Masters of their ships in the harbour to display their flags half mast high.

THAT, as a further demonstration of our grief for his loss and our respect and affection for his memory, such of the citizens as may, consistently with their peculiar religious principles, will wear black crape round their left arm for thirty days.

THAT a copy of the proceedings of this meeting be

transmitted by the Chairman to the Mayor of the city of New-York — and that the sincere and heart-felt condolence of the citizens of Philadelphia, Southwark, and the Northern Liberties, be tendered to him and to his fellow-citizens, for the loss which the state of New-York and the United States of America, have sustained in the death of General HAMILTON.

THAT a committee be appointed to carry the foregoing resolutions into effect, and to make such further arrangements relative thereto, as may be suitable to the occasion; and that the following gentlemen compose the committee:

JOHN C. STOCKER, Thomas Fitzsimons, Geo. Latimer, Elias Boudinot, Jacob Sperry, John K. Kelmuth, Godfrey Haga, Joseph Marsh, Thomas Haskins, William Lewis, William Rawle, Manuel Eyre, and Joseph Grice.

AND, that the proceedings of this meeting be subscribed by the Chairman and Secretary, and published in all the papers of the city.

THOMAS WILLING, *Chairman.*
Attest, WM. MEREDITH, *Sec'ry.*

AT a meeting of the Members of the Bar of the city of Philadelphia, held at the Court-house, on Monday, the 16th of July instant, the following resolutions were unanimously adopted:—

Resolved, That, uniting in the general grief for the

death of ALEXANDER HAMILTON, we feel it our duty to testify our deep regret for his loss, as a member of the profession to which he had returned, after a series of public labours, in which the eminence he attained was only surpassed by the variety of his excellence; in which exalted genius, incessant industry, and disinterested patriotism, enlightened and defended, enriched and dignified a nation which must ever feel for him the strongest obligations of gratitude, affection, and regret.

IN the general testimony of sorrow, we claim the right of adding our peculiar tribute, and of deploring the loss which the science of Jurisprudence, selected by him for the concluding employment of his valuable life, has sustained by his untimely and unexpected end.

Resolved, That the Members of the Bar in the city of Philadelphia, in testimony of their sorrow for the death of ALEXANDER HAMILTON, Counsellor at Law, will respectively wear black crape on their hats, for the space of thirty days.

    JARED INGERSOLL, *Chairman.*
    JOS. HOPKINSON, *Sec'ry.*

AT a meeting of the Students at Law, in the city of Philadelphia, convened at the county Court-house the 16th inst. for the purpose of adopting proper measures to testify their respect for the memory of ALEXANDER HAMILTON, Esquire, Counsellor at Law:

It was unanimously Resolved — That having long contemplated the virtues and talents of ALEXANDER HAM-

ILTON, as a bright and eminent object of imitation, they sincerely deplore the loss which they and their country have sustained, in being deprived of his example.

THAT as a memorial of the lively sensibility which has been excited by his death, they will wear black crape on their hats for thirty days.

JOHN E. HALL, *Chairman.*
GEO. CLYMER, junr. *Secretary.*

IN consequence of the intelligence of General HAMILTON's death, the bells of Christ Church were muffled on Saturday and yesterday: and the colours of the shipping in the harbour were displayed, on Saturday, at half mast.

THE Gazettes of Philadelphia were distinguished on this occasion by the heartfelt effusions of sorrow, which they contained. The following extracts from the Political Register, are eminently entitled to notice for their elegance, their pathos, and their discrimination. The two first are from the pen of the editor, Major Jackson, who was a fellow soldier with Hamilton, in our revolutionary war. The last, it will be seen, is from a correspondent.

FROM THE POLITICAL REGISTER.

THE mail from New-York of this morning, confirms the melancholy, the heart-rending intelligence of the DEATH of Gen. HAMILTON. The mourning countenance of our citizens — the anguish of his friends — the tears of his countrymen, proclaim their sense of his worth, and offer a just tribute of gratitude to his memory. To the honour of our character, let it be recorded, that those who entertained unceasing jealousy of his superior powers, while living — with honourable feeling lament him dead. After WASHINGTON, (who alone surpassed him) — after the first of Men and greatest of heroes, who has rivalled HAMILTON in usefulness to our country? — in attachment to its interests? — in unceasing labour, in the exertion of the most splendid talents for its welfare? The generous and gallant SOLDIER, the wise and virtuous STATESMAN, the eloquent and accomplished ORATOR, the ardent and magnanimous PATRIOT, has fallen the victim of unyielding honour, and inflexible integrity.

HIS memory is embalmed in the esteem and affection of his contemporaries, and will be consecrated by the gratitude of his country to future ages.

THUS hath fallen, prematurely fallen, the HERO, to whose military ardour and accomplishments America confessed the highest obligation; the CIVILIAN, from whose luminous and correct mind proceeded that invaluable commentary on the Constitution of the United States, which essentially contributed to insure its adoption; the STATESMAN, to whose talents we are indebted for the organization of our finances, and the establishment of our public credit; the JURIST and the SCHOLAR, whose combination of intellectual powers formed the boast and ornament of our country; the PATRIOT, who gave, with glowing zeal, to that country, the increasing efforts of his superior mind; and the MAN, who, endeared to his friends by every tender and ennobled quality of the heart, received in return the truest affection, and the most respectful esteem.

SAME PAPER.

When we say that Hamilton is dead! we can add nothing to the cause of grief. — When we remember how he lived, we can add nothing to the lustre of his fame. Eulogium sinks languid on the swelling heart; it gives no throb unfelt before, it cites no worth unknown. If the pathetic voice of Cicero were to speak, even from the gloom of the tomb, it could open no new source of regret, it could raise no new emotion of sorrow. Deep and solemn is the grief of a people — the tide swells from ten thousand fountains: the torrent rolls in a resistless course. If the great Spirit of our departed glory will linger but a little, and delay its ardent flight to the prepared mansions of eternal bliss, it will witness that we are not ungrateful, it will behold the pure and convulsive tributes of unaffected wo. His virtues are reflected from countless tears; and men say he is lost! as if nothing was left. The great Hope of the nation is sunk. — Party rage is overwhelmed in the flood of lamentation, and all men unite in unfeigned eulogiums on the splendid talents, the pure patriotism, the spotless integrity, the noble, disinterested nature of the lost Hamilton!

SAME PAPER.

The deplorable termination of Gen. Hamilton's career of usefulness to his country, and glory to himself, has excited, among all denominations of our fellow-citizens, those strong emotions of sympathy and grief, which his long and faithful public services, his great and splendid talents, his firm and inflexible integrity, his active and undaunted bravery, his noble, disinterested, and magnanimous patriotism, demanded from a just and grateful people.

The soldier of the Revolution laments, in deep affliction, the loss of the Hero, who was the generous and affectionate friend of his youth — the unwearied and gallant associate of his toils and dangers — and under whose auspices the honour and glory of our country never would have faded, nor its independence and happiness have ever been subverted.

The Agriculturist, the Merchant, and the Artificer, regret, with unaffected concern, the death of the Statesman, by whose indefatigable labour, and exalted genius, our finances were restored to order and arrangement; public credit was established; commerce invigorated; manufactures revived; and the means of our present unexampled prosperity, and growing greatness, brought into full and active operation.

The lawyer deplores the loss of a brother Civilian, the purity of whose professional life, in all the rage for party defamation, has never been questioned — whose eloquence and learning had neither rival nor detractor — whose talents never were exerted in the cause of injustice — never yielded to the insolence of power, nor justified the practice of oppression.

The friend of science mourns over our privation of the Scholar, whose mind was the seat of the highest intellectual endowments — whose genius had penetrated the inmost recesses of literature, and whose imagination was as brilliant and vigorous, as his judgment was intuitively strong.

The Moralist and the Christian, while indignant at the powerful, but wicked and barbarous laws, which custom has prescribed and sanctioned, weep over the lamentable sacrifice, which a high and delicate sense of honour, a pure and ennobled regard to fame and reputation, have yielded to jealousy and resentment.

The liberal and patriotic Ministerialist, with what ardour and violence he may have opposed the Founder of Federal politics, while living, is yet grieved, sincerely grieved, that our nation should be deprived of powers which conferred honour upon man.

And the Federalist, who has long listened with wonder and delight, to the just precepts of political science which have issued from his lips — who has surrendered to his wisdom and integrity, the post of his Protector, and most influential of his advisers, is overpowered with anguish for his friend — and sinks into despondence for his country.

AMICUS.

The editors of the United States Gazette, long known as the leading federal paper of the Middle States, expressed themselves in the following beautiful and energetic language.

When a great man falls, his nation mourns. When a great man and a political father falls, in the midst of his days ; " in his full strength ;" in the very vigour of his age ; at the noontide of his usefulness ; his bereaved nation suffers deep affliction. When such a man falls, aside from the ordinary course of nature ; cut off by the hand of violence; and sent suddenly, and prematurely, to be numbered with the silent dead ; his fall is yet more deeply and peculiarly bewailed — Such a man has fallen in our nation — Such a man, such a father, was Alexander Hamilton; and in such a manner has he fallen; in the midst of his days; "in his full strength;" in the very vigour of his age; at the noontide of his usefulness; cut off, alas! by the hand of violence. His fall is very deeply and peculiarly bewailed by his mourning country. Of the independence of the nation, he was a bold asserter, a brave champion; of her invaluable constitution, a most able expositor and defender; of her infantine prosperity, political and commercial, a most assiduous and successful promoter; of her maturity, the pride, the boast, the brilliant ornament; of her future hopes, the darling object; — of hopes, alas! how fatally disappointed! how suddenly, how prematurely blasted!

A CORRESPONDENT of Mr. Poulson, in the American Daily Advertiser, thus eloquently vents his grief:

OUR Hamilton, alas! is no more. Hamilton! the pride and ornament of his country, now sleeps in the tomb. We have lost him in the meridian of his days. Those resplendent abilities which gave lustre to our nation, have sunk, prematurely sunk, into the grave. The luminous and expanded intellect, so often the theme of our admiration, and our praise, is no longer to instruct and delight us. That eloquence to which Courts and Senates have listened with rapture, is for ever done. His bereaved country, in humble submission to the will of Heaven, will bear, yet mourn their loss. They will cherish the recollection of the exalted energies of his mind, of the endearing attributes of his heart. They will consecrate his memory by their sorrows and their tears. We are often called upon to deplore the loss of men, whose amiable qualities have endeared them to the circle of their private friends. When the Hero falls, the tears of his country fall with him. The statesman, the senator, and the patriot, spread by their death a general affliction. But it is our lot to bear the aggravated grief that arises at the loss of all these characters. HAMILTON, beloved by his friends, endeared to his family; the statesman, the senator, the patriot, the hero, is gone. At the fall of such a man, grief is silent, and eloquence muses eulogiums which cannot be expressed.

THE citizens of New-York, in a manner honourable to the character of our country, have upon this occasion forgotten their political distinctions, and all joined in demonstrations of sorrow at departed greatness. The presses in that city under the conduct and support of the political adversaries of General Hamilton, announce his death with appropriate lamentation. Citizens of Philadelphia, citizens of America! you will all share in the testimonies of grief at departed genius. The solemn and affecting death of the zealous defender of your revolution, of the companion in arms of your WASHINGTON, of the eloquent expounder of your constitution, claims a general mourning.

THE Port Folio thus introduces the subject:

> " IMPERIAL HONOUR's awful hand
> Shall point his lonely bed.

THIS morning intelligence of the death of Major General ALEXANDER HAMILTON has saddened this city, and will long afflict the nation. He was killed by the *Vice-*

President of the United States in a duel, fought on the Jersey shore, on the morning of the 11th of July. Whether General Hamilton was, or was not, a victim to private malignity, fomented by party rancour, his untimely death will be permanently regretted by every American who remembers the signal services, both in the cabinet and in the field, which this accomplished Scholar, this valiant Soldier, this SAGACIOUS STATESMAN, has rendered to a country, which, without his courage and counsels, would have long since mouldered into insignificance, or maddened into anarchy."

AT the conclusion of the article Mr. Dennie breaks forth in the following elegant strain of lamentation:

THUS has perished, in the prime of life, and in the midst of his usefulness, ALEXANDER HAMILTON, *the man of exalted sentiments, and extensive views*, whose theories guided the statesman, whose *eloquence influenced senates*, whose *delicacy might have polished courts*, and whose versatile talents blessed mankind. He has fallen, not in the course of nature, not jeopardizing his life in the high places of the field, but by a private and petty hand — and his perplexed and sorrowing country makes the pathetic interrogatory of the royal Psalmist:

KNOW YE NOT THAT THERE IS A GREAT MAN FALLEN THIS DAY IN ISRAEL?

UPON opening the General's will, there was found enclosed in it a letter to his wife, written on the 4th inst. in which he tells her, that he had endeavoured, by all possible means, to avoid the duel, but that he found it impossible, unless by acting in a manner which would justly forfeit her esteem. That he should certainly fall, and she would receive that letter after his death. He begs her forgiveness for being the cause of so much pain to her, and earnestly entreated her to bear herself up under that load of grief with which she would be overwhelmed, placing a firm reliance on a kind Providence who would never desert her.

THE subsequent Port Folio was entirely devoted to the subject. This paper (says Mr. Dennie) is consecrated to the Memorial of ALEXANDER HAMILTON, of whose afflicted Country, bereaved of her brightest, greatest, and most stedfast hope, it may be appropriately said, in the words of an eloquent ancient,

> Quæ cum magna modis multis miranda videtur,
> Gentibus humanis regio, visenda fertur,
> Rebus opima bonis, multâ munita virûm vi,
> NIL *tamen*, HOC *habuisse* viro præclarius *in se*
> Nec sanctum magis et carumque videtur.

[THEN follows the correspondence, accompanied by the letter of Bishop Moore; to which are subjoined the "funeral obsequies," the "funeral oration," and the best written eulogiums that have appeared in the various papers. The following paragraphs, from Mr. Dennie's own polished hand, close " the memorial."]

THE elegant encomium, with the signature of "AMICUS," which we reprint from the Register, is an eloquent and affectionate tribute to the memory of the illustrious dead. We add, with peculiar pleasure, that with one disgraceful and infamous exception, the editors of the daily papers of Philadelphia have manifested their respect for the memory of Hamilton, in panegyric the most pathetic, liberal, ingenious, and sincere.

With respect to the city at large, its grief has been, by no means, limited in extent, or feeble in expression. Thrusting aside, as unworthy consideration, the rancorous jacobin, the scoffing deist, the *snivelling fanatic*, and the imported scoundrel, we have heard the voice of deep lament from *every side*. All, *who have a tear for pity*, all good and true men, all *genuine* Patriots, the votaries of Christianity, the votaries of Genius, every magnanimous, every virtuous individual, have bewailed the private loss, and *the public calamity*. On the Saturday, when this national misfortune was first reported in the city, the Editor, as he took his melancholy rounds, was struck with the contemplation of the general anxiety; and when he beheld those who wept for the fall of Hamilton, and those "who were *indignant at its cause*," he could not avoid remembering a picturesque description by a great historical Painter. "Neque populi aut *plebis* ulla vox; sed attoniti vultus, et conversæ ad omnia aures. Non tumultus, non quies; sed quale magni metus et MAGNÆ IRÆ silentium est."

We have remarked, with signal satisfaction, that with very few exceptions, the respectable Society of Friends have testified a sincere regret for the hapless lot of Hamilton. Though their peculiar tenets preclude a *Sad Ostent*, in memory of the dead; though they wear no *inky cloaks nor customary suits of solemn black*, yet theirs is the sagacity to discern the value of a great Statesman, and theirs is the silent sorrow which muses at his loss.

*** The friends of the Editor are very respectfully notified, that the publication of the Port Folio has been postponed that he might present a complete and accurate view of a most sinister event, which has overwhelmed America with affliction. Notwithstanding his utmost pains, and his fervent zeal to exhibit all that is plausive and respectful of that *greatness* and *goodness*, so conspicuous in the character of General Hamilton, it is apprehended some omission or some error may appear from the very eagerness of the Editor to do ample justice to the subject. Hereafter, the column of HAMILTON'S FAME may be indicated by no random or feeble hand. Meanwhile, I thus remember the pathetic prophecy of the classic Historian, which TACITUS has not applied with more truth to Julius Agricola, than it may be applied to Alexander Hamilton.

QUIDQUID ex illo amavimus, quidquid mirati sumus, MANET, MANSURUMQUE est in animis hominum, fama rerum. Nam multos veterum velut inglorios et ignobiles oblivio obruet. *Ille*, Posteritati narratus et traditus, SUPERSTES ERIT.

EXTRACTS will now be indiscriminately presented from various other papers in the order they appeared. They will all serve to show, that the tears which flowed on the death of Hamilton were not confined to a few men, nor to a particular party; but that it was the nation who wept for his loss.

THE following eminently beautiful lines, marked equally by delicacy and pathos, first appeared in the American Citizen. We presume from the signature, they are from the pen of Mrs. R——, a Lady whose effusions have sometimes heretofore adorned the columns of the Morning Chronicle.

THE GRAVE OF HAMILTON.

Soft beam thy rays, fair daughter of the skies,
With rich profusion gilding o'er this scene
Of deep repose and death: each vagrant breeze
Lies hush'd within its cell, in seeming fear
The solemn calm of nature should be broken —
Save when a solitary zephyr's sound,
Sighing, in mournful cadence, thro' the trees,
Seems like a parted spirit's whisp'ring voice
Which tells of wo to come —
A chilly horror rushes thro' my frame,
As o'er this sad sepulchral scene I tread,
With slow and winding step — lest on some grave
Haste might impel my feet — Nor you, ye wise,
Smile at the superstition fond, which deems
The act unholy, and a sacrilege
To nature's laws: Oh! rather join and pay
The rev'rence due to nature's sad remains.
This is the spot my wand'ring feet have sought,
The last receptacle of him, who once
Was great and good — alas! how far beyond
The reach of common natures: his it was
To blend each nobler quality which forms
The soldier, statesman, and endearing friend,
In happy union — his the feeling heart,
Which to the tender charities of life
Beat in kind unison — th' electric power
Of Genius was his own, in such degree
That all stood mute before him. Awful lesson
To man's fond vanity — that Hamilton,
Whose wisdom, goodness, valour, were almost
Beyond all parallel, has bow'd beneath
Death's iron sceptre; and but late entomb'd
That eye, whose lightning spoke the soul within;
Those lips, whose sounds in pleasing fetters held
Each ear attentive, mouldering in the dust. —
Bright dart the moon-beams o'er his lowly grave,
And, by their silv'ry light, methinks I read

A name to him allied — his eldest Hope !
Heart-piercing sight ! here, side by side arrang'd,
Father and Son lie wrapt in long repose !
Alike untimely fallen, victims alike
To honour — Tyrant of the feeling heart.
Oh, hapless mother ! widow'd wife ! what words
Can paint thine anguish ? Scarce the streaming tears
Which deep maternal sorrow taught to flow,
Were dry'd from thy pale cheek, when this rude blow
Struck at the beam of peace that still remain'd,
And tore it from thy breast. May each blest power,
Kind guardians of the good, with constant care
Support thy grief-worn heart; and resignation
Upon thy bosom shed her healing dew.
For him, who lies this sacred dust beneath,
Vain is our deep regret — a nation's tears,
A nation's prayers, could not avail to add
One moment to his life : Yet to ourselves,
A soothing, melancholy pleasure springs,
From ev'ry tribute render'd to his worth —
How justly all must know. Fond mem'ry still
Delights to trace the youthful warrior's steps
From field to field; but chiefly loves to dwell
On southern plains, where York extends her bounds;
Where, to the desp'rate charge his troops he led,
Then on the vanquish'd foe benignly smil'd.
Sure angels, from their bright abodes, look'd down,
And blest a vict'ry worthy of a hero.
Unmark'd with blood's contaminating stain,
Valour and Mercy, for his youthful brow,
A laurel crown entwin'd with fairest flowers
Perennial intermix'd — still shall it bloom,
Tho' "cold and motionless " the hand that won it,
And to remotest ages give its sweets.
But why recount his deeds in war or peace ?
O'er all Columbia's wide extended shores
His name, long since, was heard. Who did not know
In worth and valour few were found his equals —
In genius, none ? Then, be his well-earned fame
Confided to a grateful people's care.

            CLARA.

THE ALBANY CENTINEL.

THOSE Citizens of Albany who are desirous of uniting to express their sorrow and regret at the loss our country has suffered in the death of one of its firmest citizens, ALEXANDER HAMILTON, are requested to meet at the City-Hall, at six o'clock this evening.

CITY OF ALBANY.

At a Common Council held in and for the City of Albany, at the City-Hall of the said city, on the 17*th day of July,* 1804:

THE Common Council having heard with extreme regret, the untimely and afflicting death of Major-General ALEXANDER HAMILTON:

Resolved unanimously, That as a tribute of respect to the memory of that exalted and most worthy man, the members of the Common Council and the Officers of this Corporation, will wear a mourning crape on the left arm for the space of six weeks.

Extract from the minutes of the Common Council,
RICHARD LUSH, *President.*

At a meeting of the Albany Military Association, at Lewis's City Tavern, *on the* 17*th July,* 1804,

Lieut. Col. VAN SCHAICK, *President:*

THE Association convened for the purpose of paying a suitable testimony of respect to the memory of Major-General Alexander Hamilton — in whose death our

Country has to deplore the loss of a Patriot, a Statesman, and a Soldier; our State, a dignified and illustrious Citizen; and genius, honour, and humanity, one of their brightest ornaments:

Resolved unanimously, That the Members of this Association will wear Crape as mourning for Major-General Alexander Hamilton, deceased, for the space of six weeks, and also on the first company parade and regimental review.

Extract from the minutes,
JOHN WILLARD, *Secretary.*

THE ALBANY REGISTER. (*Democratic.*)

In our last we mentioned slightly, that Gen. Hamilton had been mortally wounded in a duel with Col. Burr. This melancholy intelligence has since been confirmed, to the deep regret of all who admire genius, respect talents, or revere a dignified spirit of honour and integrity: such was the spirit which animated the soul of Hamilton, and which commanded for his personal character the veneration of all classes of citizens, not excepting the most decided of his political enemies: with these we have ever ranked; but this consideration shall not check the expression of our feelings. Who is there, that will not mourn the loss of a man whose unrivalled eloquence alone rendered him the ornament of his profession, and the pride of his country? As a politician we did not regard him; but as an exalted genius, as an eloquent, brave, generous, frank, and honourable man, we shall ever lament his loss and revere his memory.

THE TRENTON FEDERALIST.

IN this day's Gazette we present our readers with the interesting correspondence between Gen. Hamilton and Col. Burr, preceding the fatal rencounter which has deprived our country of one of its brightest ornaments. While we lament the supposed necessity which called the venerable deceased to the field of death, we should unite our griefs and mingle our tears with the thousands who are deeply bewailing the severe, and perhaps we might add irreparable, loss. Another of the heroes of our revolution, another of the founders of our republic, has been hurried to the tomb : Another of the pillars of our commonwealth has been tumbled into ruins. Since the departure of our WASHINGTON, the death of no man has excited such general grief, or covered our country with so general a mourning. Even those who were, while he lived, his political adversaries, seem to have buried their opposition in his grave, and many of them, lamenting the loss which their country and society have sustained, place themselves among the foremost to pay every tribute of respect to his splendid merits and transcendent abilities. Alas ! Hamilton, the sage, the soldier, and the patriot, is no more ! In the vigour of years, and in the midst of eminent usefulness, he has gone to the mansions of the dead. Over his ashes it becomes the country he has served with such devoted zeal, such inflexible integrity, and such prosperous success, to raise some splendid memorial which shall bid future generations venerate his name, and emulate his attachment to the public welfare. But ah ! when we reflect that no monument marks the spot where repose the ashes of our Washington, we fear this testimonial of gratitude must be left to other times. — Like him, however, he has raised for himself a monument which shall defy the blast of ages to tarnish, or the corroding tooth of time to deface. Light be the sod which lies upon his breast! Green be the grass which grows upon his grave! Eternal be the laurels which flourish round his tomb!

THE FEDERAL ARK.

IT is recommended to our fellow-citizens of Delaware, that, following the example of their brethren of New-York and Philadelphia, they wear crape on the left arm for thirty days, in honour of the late General HAMILTON.

TIME has been gathering to the tomb the heroes and sages of our revolution, and HAMILTON, with his blushing honours thick upon him, has yielded to its omnipotent sway.

WHEN he fell, the Genius of America, recollecting with gratitude, and swelling with grief, shed a tear to his memory, which blotted out for ever the imperfections of the man from the brilliant record of his virtues.

OUR tutelary genius presided at his birth. — Nature was his foster-mother. — Virtue blushed not to call him her son. — Wisdom claimed him as her favourite son. — Patriotism with rapture pressed him to her bosom, and Valour by her side, smiling on her caresses, resolved to complete the man. Enrolled in the list of our heroes, thy name, HAMILTON, shall never be forgotten. As a great man, in common with the world, we admired; in the circle of the private citizen we loved thee; and, as a champion in the cause of our liberty, we know not how to express to thee our gratitude.

THE electric shock has appalled and paralyzed the country. Party spirit forgoes its rancour; commerce, with its busy step, forgets its course; the great and small alike pay the tribute of a tear, and feel, in the loss of HAMILTON, a national calamity. Obeying, then, the impulse of our own feelings, let us join our fellow-citizens in paying the last sad tribute to his memory.

A FRIEND TO DEPARTED MERIT.

MR. COLEMAN,
If the following are not entirely unworthy of their exalted subject, give them a place in the Evening Post.
A.

VERSES

ON THE DEATH OF GENERAL HAMILTON.

SOLDIERS of Freedom! veil your eyes,
For low in dust your leader lies:
No more his gleaming steel he draws,
The foremost in his country's cause.

PATRIOTS! who in the rolls of fame,
Have nobly earn'd a glorious name;
With melting grief your loss deplore —
The Second Washington's no more!

YE Children of Columbia! weep —
Your Statesman's lock'd in death's long sleep;
And, till the course of time has roll'd,
His like you never shall behold.

OFFSPRING of feeling! o'er his bier
Heave the swoln sigh, and drop the tear —
For others' wo, *his eyes* knew well
To pour their streams — *his breast* to swell.

POOR widow'd and dejected land!
Where canst thou find, like *his*, a hand

To prop the fabric of thy state,
And shield thee, like o'er-ruling fate?
WELL may'st thou grieve, and hang thy head —
Thy *boast*, thy *guardian pow'r*, is fled.
Oh! why, e'er Heav'n reclaim'd his mind,
Was not his " mantle " left behind?

THE following lines, considered as the production of a young Miss, only twelve years of age, a favourite of General Hamilton's in his life time, will be read with some interest:

ELEGY,

ON THE DEATH OF GEN. HAMILTON.

HARK! while the deep-toned, solemn, funeral bell,
Proclaims some Chief has bade the world farewell!
Mark! how they pay to worth the tribute due,
While pitying tears the mournful cheek bedew.
Well may they weep, and for his loss deplore:
His country's friend, great Hamilton's no more!
Who will not sigh when virtue meets the doom,
And generous worth is summon'd to the tomb?
But in the feeling mind he'll ne'er expire,
Still crouds shall bless him — blessing, still admire;
Still shall he live, the favourite of Fame,
Who thro' the world shall sound his honour'd name;
Record the virtues in his soul combin'd,
True to his friends, nor to his foes unkind;
Candid as truth, like innocence sincere,
Liberal and just, when other's faults appear;
And when an error, or a vice he found,
He scorn'd to add reproaches to the wound.
When he fought nobly in his country's cause,
'T was not ambition of a vain applause,
But from pure motives, like a patriot brave,
Her rights, her laws, her liberties, to save —
Shall, then, Columbia's sons their grief repress?

Shall they not all their virtuous hero bless?
Who is there now can unconcern'd appear,
And from his memory withhold the tear?
See, at the tomb, what mournful crouds attend,
Oh! patriot, hero, husband, father, friend!
Now free from cares, from mad revenge secure,
Angels shall waft thee to those regions pure,
Where worth like thine shall find its bright reward,
And FACTION's murd'rous arm is never rear'd.

L. L.

THE NEW-HAVEN VISITOR.

THE painful task this day devolves on us of announcing to our readers an event at once awful and distressing. The illustrious ALEXANDER HAMILTON IS NO MORE! He expired on Thursday last, of a wound received the preceding day, in a duel with Col. Burr. This fatal duel, which has deprived the world of so great and distinguished a character, originated, we understand, not from any particular cause, but from a long course of political animosity.

SAME PAPER.

WE presume our readers will pardon us for engrossing this day's paper with accounts of the tragic scene in New-York. We have endeavoured to present the most important parts of the whole to them, that they may, with one view, behold the deplorable consequences inseparable from a custom that sets at defiance the laws of God and man, and is as barbarous as vicious.

IT appears that the cause of this for ever to be lamented duel was of no great moment. The scene is opened with a trifle apparently as "light as air;" but soon becomes deeply interesting and affecting. Its progress is marked with death, a funeral, and bitterest weeping. — In it we behold the Vice-President, the second Magistrate of five millions of people, in direct contempt of all law, all morality, all religion, and apparently without any just provocation, raise his hand against, and deliberately destroy, the life of one of our first and most distinguished characters — a character who would do honour to any country, to any age, and who could not die without a nation wept. — Let us imagine this venerable man, this great victim of false honour, bleeding before us. — See,

> " Rolled in blood he gasping lies ;
> Too daring " man ; pride's " noblest sacrifice :
> His snow-white bosom heaves with writhing pain,
> The purple drops his snow white bosom stain ;
> His cheeks of rose are wan ; a deadly hue
> Sits on his face that chills with lucid dew ;
> Swiftly his colour flies, he groans, he dies ! "

—— Yes, he dies, but his well-earned fame will never die. It will ever be held in remembrance by his grateful country.

AMONG the papers, federal or democratic, which have done themselves honour by their manner of speaking of the late melancholy event, we particularly distinguish the National Ægis. The following elegant extract is from the pen of some gentleman who occasionally assists in writing for this print.

THE NATIONAL ÆGIS.

Death of General Hamilton. — The last Southern mails have brought to us a melancholy confirmation of this distressing intelligence. On Wednesday the 11th inst. at 8 o'clock in the morning, he received a mortal wound in a duel with Col. Burr, and expired the day following, at 2 o'clock ! The particulars, so far as they have transpired, will be found under the New-York head. The papers of that city having observed a cautious and gloomy silence on this occasion, it is not in our power to satisfy the curiosity of our readers, by detailing all the dreadful circumstances of this disaster. Enough, however, is developed, to awaken the sensibility, and to excite the keenest anguish of all those who are disposed to forget the lighter shades of political difference, in the overwhelming distresses of their fellow-creatures.

We notice, with pride and satisfaction, the arrangements which had been made among all classes of people, of whatever profession or party, in the city of which he was an illustrious inhabitant, to render a feeling and unequivocal testimony of esteem for his character, of regret for his death, and respect for his memory. Personal resentment has been soothed, private animosity has been forgotten, and the spirit of party has been lulled to repose, by the contemplation of this calamitous event.

The patriot, to whatever political sect he may belong, remembers in him, the firm, the enlightened, the profound, the inflexible *Statesman*. The soldier looks back, with grateful devotion, on his revolutionary labours, and reveres the intrepid friend and companion of "*our first and greatest revolutionary hero.*" The man of letters mourns, with milder sorrow, the learned philosopher, and the accomplished scholar!—The admirer of eloquence dwells with rapture on the musical accents of his voice, the beautiful sublimity of his language, and the irresistible force of his persuasion!—He who delights in the blandishments of life, and finds comfort and consolation in the enjoyments of social intercourse, cannot withhold a tear when he calls to his mind the amiable and interesting traits in his character, which had won the affection of all, who were comprised within the extended circle of his acquaintance! — His family — But here, remembrance is too painful! — Within the narrow compass of two years — a wife and a mother has followed to the grave, a son and a husband; both victims to the same cruel and untimely destiny! — The annals of our Country do not record an instance of parallel distress! We forbear to harrow up her soul by cold and unfeeling reflections on the manner of his death! — If an inveterate and deep-rooted custom is ever to be exploded, it will be done, not by the labours of the moralist, or the threatenings of the preacher : Scenes of such poignant affliction will sink deep on the memory, and will serve as an awful warning to the followers of that treacherous Phantom, which leads to beguile, and seduces to destroy.

FOR THE EVENING POST.

AN IRREGULAR ODE.

Hark ! how the passing bell
Heaves to the gale its sullen swell :
And lo ! in sorrow's pomp array'd,
   To the dull beat of death,
The slowly moving cavalcade !
   The half-suspended breath
Scarce frees the struggling sigh !
And hallow'd tears bedew mute Beauty's eye —
Now, o'er the mansions of the dead,
Behold the solemn measur'd tread !
Around their slumb'ring Hero drawn,
The silent Soldiers print the lawn —
     Now the long blaze
     Arrests the gaze ;

The hollow vaults resound —
  The blazing sky,
The thund'ring ground ;
  The stedfast eye,
More eloquent than Pity's flow,
Proclaims the Soldier's manly wo.
High o'er the scene the curling cloud aspires,
  Fraught with a nation's fervid sighs
  The mighty incense seeks the skies,
And Heav'n approves the scene — for Hamilton expires !

[In compliance with the wishes of the public here, Mr. Nott's Discourse will make part of the next number.]

END OF NO. II.

A COLLECTION, &c.

N°. III.

FROM THE FREDERICK-TOWN HERALD.

Death of General Hamilton. — On this day it is but decent, and indeed our emotions would oblige us, to muffle the rude voice of dissention and party conflict, in the mournful task of condoling with our country on a calamity, which nothing but the loss of her beloved Washington could exceed, and no other visitation could equal. With inexpressible grief, with a heart overflowing with sorrow, and sunk and depressed under a sense of the common affliction, we have to present a confirmation of the sad tidings that General Hamilton is no more! That our Hero and Patriot, our Statesman and Orator, the Benefactor of this nation and the Stay of her best and last hopes, the admiration of Europe, whose glorious eminence and combination of glories, nor Europe nor the World can this day surpass, that our Pride, our Boast, and our Dependence, is taken from us, "gone to his death bed," " fallen by too severe a fate," cut off in the prime of his maturity and the fulness of all his excellence! —

"But the course of this orb, though marked, was short. It is set; never to return! — Thou sleepest the sleep of death! But we are not unmindful of thee, O Achilles; in life and in death thou art equally the object of our regard and veneration!"

On such an occasion, and at such a moment as this, deep distress but chokes invention, and would fain borrow utterance for the last melancholy office. Casting our eyes on the space held by the very first man of all this land, and the great void which his sudden and deplorable fate now leaves, we can only apply the words of Edmund Burke in the ardour of his feelings for the loss of Johnson — " He has made a chasm which not only nothing can fill up, but which nothing has a tendency to fill up — Hamilton is dead — Let us go to the next best — There is nobody — No man can be said to put you in mind of Hamilton." — And still dwelling on his acknowledged superiority in whatever is honourable to our nature, with a full allowance for the general imperfections of that nature, and an admission of every infirmity particularly attributable to him, we may further use the concluding sentiment of Burke's own biographer, that, "With little alloy, and so much sterling value, in realms in which great talents are frequent, and great virtues not rare, in the usual course of intellectual and practical excellence, centuries may pass before Providence again bestow an" Alexander Hamilton.

The affecting manner in which his untimely end is announced on all sides, and every where heard, and in which all parties and all classes in the city of New-York have joined in public sympathy and lamentation, and the pomp of funeral honours, now " canonizes and sanctifies a character," which it was the purpose of Washington, in one of the last acts of his life, to record above all others. The truly Christian manner of his dying, will also interest every tender and virtuous mind ; and a more authentic account than the letter among the extracts here subjoined, will be impatiently looked for to explain the unfortunate circumstances which led to that death, in his duel with the Vice-President, Col. Burr, on Wednesday the 11th inst. upon the Jersey shore: where, by a like catastrophe, but two years since, the grave robbed him of a son, and blasted all his fond expectation just as the bud of youthful promise was opening into the bloom of manhood. Such a statement, it will be perceived, is expected in the Evening Post of Mr. Coleman, than whom no man perhaps, out of the weeping and bereft family of his illustrious friend, can more fervently bewail that loss which he knows so well how to appreciate. We shall deem it a duty to communicate whatever appears on this unhappy subject, of a nature to satisfy anxiety, or to afford consolation under the most awful and irreparable blow, which it was possible for a people to sustain.

SAME PAPER.

O AMERICA! veil thyself in black! — Deep mourns the Eagle, with shattered wing, in some lone spot — its gayest plumage lost — the favourite, o'er whom it was wont to hover, one cruel blow has severed from the world. The tears of the aged burst forth — the withered hand trembles in grief — the youthful patriots mourn — Their Chief is fallen! — Haste! even now he bleeds! — he dies! — Catch the stream that flows from his mighty heart, and pour it in thy veins — Cultivate the laurel for his memory, and earn a sprig to grace thy manly brows. In bliss above, his spirit is received — the hand of mercy is stretched forth — joy rises on the soul. — Ye hosts of heaven, assemble thy chosen choir — croud round the celestial throne — raise loud the song of glory — send forth its sound on golden clarions — Behold, a WASHINGTON and a HAMILTON, again in gladness and in triumph meet. —

PASTORA.

SAME PAPER.

The National Loss.—Before resuming the mournful subject which shrouded the last *Herald*, we must relieve ourselves by expressing the uneasiness we have felt at a scrap under the name of an Anecdote, amidst our agitation inadvertently let into the same paper, with something like an appearance of levity, when our Editorial thoughts were really occupied, as indeed they still are, with nothing but sadness. For the present we have put by several communications, and given up every other subject, since that of Gen. Hamilton's death alone engrosses the public attention; nor can we help regretting, for the sake of our country readers, that our paper is not large enough to contain at full length every thing which appears of an interesting and authentic nature relative to an event, which seems to have spread with the force of an electric shock, in all directions accessible to the better feelings, or even the compunctions of humanity. Not having it in our power to republish the whole as it should be, we must be content to fill up our columns with such selections from the mass of matter in the New-York Evening Post, as may be thought most essential, noticing at the same time by way of introduction, whatever is most material in the rest.

WITH respect to the funeral honours paid the illustrious deceased, there is a melancholy satisfaction in observing with what general devotion the preparations announced in our last, have been carried into effect in the city of New-York. The burial took place on Saturday the 14th; the procession was formed agreeably to the arrangements published; and the day exhibited a scene altogether one of the most affecting in the annals of death, such as must indeed have been "enough to melt a monument of marble." According to appointment, Mr. Gouverneur Morris, oppressed and labouring under the weight of grief, delivered the extempore address, which is the first article now republished in compliance with the expectations excited last week. In addition to what was done in New-York on the 14th, we must not pass by the tribute of grateful remembrance rendered by the citizens of Philadelphia, by several public bodies and Societies in both cities, by the Societies of Cincinnati generally, and particularly the resolutions of the Cincinnati of New-York, condoling with the afflicted Widow of their President-General, cherishing his fame with the balm of affection, and as a lasting mark of their respect voting a Monument to his memory, with a suitable inscription, in Trinity Church. Nor can we here forbear adverting to the singular degree of kindness publicly proffered by some on the fall of this Great Man, who were most violently opposed to him while living; as if obliged now by an irresistible impulse which they cannot help, to do justice to the virtues of his heart, and the noble preeminence of his mind; and in espousing his last fatal wrong, to assert the whole tenour of his goodness, and defend him even from themselves. It is even impossible to attest his glory in stronger language, than that used in Cheetham's American Citizen, where General Hamilton is represented (in the words) "most perfect." In such instances, we would fain consider the *present* as sincere, and we would try to forget the *past*.

RELATIVE to the causes which have produced all this mourning, the expected statement is now also given to the public. The correspondence which shows the cause of the duel, together with the General's observations left sealed up with his will, will be duly considered by the public. As to what passed on the ground, the short account which follows is all that the seconds of the parties have been able to agree upon. With respect to a material fact or two, whether General Hamilton fired *at* Col. Burr, or meant to fire at all, it seems there has been a difference of opinion. But we think every body must acknowledge that Gen. Hamilton's friend, Judge Pendleton, has put the matter beyond all doubt in the reasons he has since assigned for his opinion; and Col. Burr's second, Mr. Van Ness, is certainly mistaken. In the paper of observations, left sealed up by Gen. Hamilton, the reader will see that he had " resolved (in case of an ' opportunity ') to *reserve* and *throw away* his first fire, and had thoughts even of *reserving* his second fire, thus giving a double opportunity to Col. Burr, to pause and reflect." The circumstances so impressively stated by Mr. Pendleton, are conclusive evidence that his determination remained unaltered. He stood exposed to suffer death from the fury of his antagonist, without an attempt to inflict it — He gave up his own life, so precious to the world, rather than offer to preserve it by aiming at the life of his destroyer. With this ill-fated magnanimity of spirit, the unrelenting malevolence to which he sunk a victim must now abide a contrast: — Col. Burr himself has the conviction to undergo, a conviction not much calculated, one would suppose, to add to his triumph or his happiness, that on a mere vague pretence of injury, he has committed the last great injury of all on a man, who, while in the very act of suffering it, was incapable of doing him harm, under the influence of those benign principles which he chose rather to ratify with his blood than to offend against.

We have said unrelenting malevolence. — We should not have said it, and thus contributed to prejudge his case, if there was any prospect of Col. Burr's becoming amenable to the laws, as he and his second ought to be. For himself he has fled to the southward, and there is no likelihood that his friend, Governor Bloomfield of New-Jersey, in which state the crime was perpetrated, will demand his being delivered up for trial. But if there ever was an instance, in which the law should take its course, this duel is one where every thing would call loudly for an example to be made. In most instances of the kind, arising from a violent provocation, or from the sudden heat of passion, in which death ensues, juries, in their indulgence for human frailty, have been apt to get over the rigour of the law, and when they could not entirely acquit, have converted the offence into manslaughter only. But if murder be, what it is defined, "an unlawful killing with *malice aforethought*, express or implied," if this constitute murder, we ask the reader to accompany us through the whole of the correspondence and narrative preceding the duel, in which the cause of quarrel is explained, and then say whether there has not been on the part of Col. Burr, "*malice aforethought*," the most "express," wanton, and implacable.

We are thus confident in our expressions, because we have seen every thing offered in his behalf by his own Second, but which does not in the least contradict the other statement; which does not indeed attempt to introduce as a document in the affair, a paper hitherto known only to Col. Burr and his Second, being a sort of communication which his Second was verbally to make (but did not make, as he admits himself in the terms used) to Gen. Hamilton, on the subject of fancied wrongs to the character of Col. Burr, from time to time supposed to proceed from Gen. Hamilton; but which communication, if it had been made, was only of a tendency to aggravate, and goes to confirm our belief of Col. Burr's " predetermined hostility," which nothing reasonable could ever satisfy or appease. — Yet, as Mr. Coleman justly remarks, "this foisting a secret, and till now an unheard-of paper, into the genuine correspondence (at least) shows in no equivocal manner, that the writer was conscious that the correspondence which really took place, presents a case no way favourable to his principal." — Indeed it is now matter of astonishment and indignation to us, how the Morning Chronicle of N. York, the paper under Col. Burr's control, should have had the audacity to assert, by way of assurance, " that when a fair and candid statement was laid before the public, the conduct of Mr. Burr would be justified by every disinterested and unprejudiced man." — But we will freely leave it to every such man to decide. For ourselves, we are convinced that had Col. Burr, in the late contest, succeeded in being elected Governor of New-York, our country would not now be deploring this tragic work of his hand: But in the sullenness and mortification of disappointment, he seems to have whetted up a desperate vengeance, which was to lower Gen. Hamilton, who it is known had not countenanced his recent pretensions with the Federalists. Else, had a jealous care of his reputation been the sole motive, why should those opponents, all the Clintons and the Livingstons, who have most openly and successfully reprobated him, have escaped his rage? If animosity for imagined insult or defiance alone prompted him, where was all his fierceness and tenacity of honour, when, in the duel with his friend Swartwout, Mr. De Witt Clinton exclaimed a wish " that he had the Principal there?" But no! " Revolving in the gloomy recesses of his mind," the resentment of Col. Burr has taken a different turn; or rather the craft of his malignity has sought a different object for its safer gratification: and thus at the very moment in which it was insisted that " Federalists, and Federalists alone, voted for Col. Burr," on his part he was plotting destruction to the main prop and hope of Federalism in these States. Surely we have some right to complain; surely this man has been destined to us for a curse, and a vexation without end. But at this moment we forget every mischief but the present; we think not of him as a chief among the original authors of our political ruin, but we start with horror from those hands now reeking with the blood of Hamilton. — This last sin has swallowed up every other. — It is a spot which nothing can wash out. — Col. Burr may, if he pleases, enjoy the glory of this transgression — but though he shares not the fate of the wretch who fired the temple of Ephesus to eternize his name, which his countrymen would never afterwards repeat; though Col. Burr will be remembered and have celebrity, it will now be, because

"*Damned* to everlasting fame."

It is impossible it should be otherwise: it is impossible we should restrain these sentiments, since we find the direful blow to have been the entire consequence and fixed purpose of his own subtle, premeditated, fiend-like rancour; pursuing without remorse, and as it were with an imprecation not to stop until he had pushed into the grave. He succeeded; the Genius of Evil was ascendant;

and the most estimable and distinguished of the survivors of Washington, the orb of transcendent lustre, the most "finished man in this exigent time," our guardian, beloved, and ever to be lamented Hamilton, fell! . . .

> "Oh what a fall was there, my Countrymen!
> "Then you and I, and all of us fell down,
> "Whilst bloody treason flourished over us."

THE following Sermon has deservedly engaged an universal share of public attention. The successful manner in which the author combats the fashionable vice of duelling, requires that his production should be extensively circulated. The distant reader will here see in what terms a Minister of God, standing before his altar, feels himself justified in speaking of the virtues, talents, and public services, of the great Hamilton. In the passage beginning with the apostrophe "*Approach and behold,*" how elegant, how deeply affecting, how sublime, is he! Perhaps a passage of equal length is not to be any where found, in our language, superior to this.

A DISCOURSE,

Delivered in the North Dutch Church, in the City of Albany, occasioned by the ever to be lamented Death of General ALEXANDER HAMILTON — *July* 29, 1804.

BY *ELIPHALET NOTT, A. M.*

PASTOR OF THE PRESBYTERIAN CHURCH IN SAID CITY.

II. SAMUEL, I. 19. — *How are the Mighty Fallen!*

THE occasion explains the choice of my subject. A subject on which I enter in obedience to your request.

You have assembled to express your elegiac sorrows, and sad and solemn weeds cover you.

BEFORE such an audience, and on such an occasion, I enter on the duty assigned me with trembling. Do not mistake my meaning. I tremble indeed — not, however, through fear of failing to merit your applause; for what have I to do with that when addressing the dying, and treading on the ashes of the dead — Not through fear of failing, justly, to portray the character of that great man who is at once the theme of my encomium and regret: He needs not eulogy. His work is finished, and death has removed him beyond my censure, and I would fondly hope, through grace, above my praise.

YOU will ask then, why I tremble? I tremble to think that I am called to attack from this place a crime, the very idea of which almost freezes one with horror — a crime, too, which exists among the polite and polished orders of society, and which is accompanied with every aggravation; committed with cool deliberation — and openly in the face of day!

BUT I have a duty to perform. And difficult and awful as that duty is, I will not shrink from it.

WOULD to God my talents were adequate to the occasion. But such as they are, I devoutly proffer them to unfold the nature and counteract the influence of that barbarous custom, which, like a resistless torrent, is undermining the foundations of civil government — breaking down the barriers of social happiness, and sweeping away virtue, talents, and domestic felicity, in its desolating course.

ANOTHER and an illustrious character — a father — a general — a statesman — the very man who stood on an eminence and without a rival, among sages and heroes, the future hope of his country in danger — this man, yielding to the influence of a custom which deserves our eternal reprobation, has been brought to an untimely end.

THAT the deaths of great and useful men should be particularly noticed, is equally the dictate of reason and revelation. The tears of Israel flowed at the decease of good JOSIAH, and to his memory the funeral women chanted the solemn dirge.

BUT neither examples nor arguments are necessary to wake the sympathies of a grateful people on such occasions. The death of public benefactors surcharges the heart, and it spontaneously disburdens itself by a flow of sorrows.

SUCH was the death of WASHINGTON: to embalm whose memory, and perpetuate whose deathless fame, we lent our feeble, but unnecessary services. Such, also, and more peculiarly so, has been the death of HAMILTON.

THE tidings of the former moved us — mournfully moved us — and we wept. The account of the latter chilled our hopes, and curdled our blood. The former died in a good old age; the latter was cut off in the midst of his usefulness. The former was a customary providence: we saw in it, if I may speak so, the finger of GOD, and rested in his sovereignty. The latter is not attended with this soothing circumstance.

THE fall of HAMILTON owes its existence to mad deliberation, and is marked by violence. The time, the place, the circumstances, are arranged with barbarous coolness. The instrument of death is levelled in daylight, and with well directed skill pointed at his heart. Alas! the event has proven that it was but too well directed. Wounded, mortally wounded, on the very spot which still smoked with the blood of a favourite son, into the arms of his indiscreet and cruel friend the father fell.

AH! had he fallen in the course of nature; or jeopardizing his life in defence of his country, had he fallen — But he did not. He fell in single combat — Pardon my mistake — he did not fall in single combat. His noble nature refused to endanger the life of his antagonist. But he exposed his own life. This was his crime: and the sacredness of my office forbids that I should hesitate explicitly to declare it so.

HE did not hesitate to declare it so himself: "My religious and moral principles are strongly opposed to duelling." These are his words before he ventured to the field of death. "I view the late transaction with sorrow and contrition." These are his words after his return.

HUMILIATING end of illustrious greatness! — *How are the mighty fallen!* And shall the mighty thus fall? Thus shall the noblest lives be sacrificed and the richest blood be spilt? *Tell it not in Gath; publish it not in the streets of Askelon!*

THINK not that the fatal issue of the late inhuman interview was fortuitous. No; the Hand that guides unseen the arrow of the archer, steadied and directed the arm of the duellist. And why did it thus direct it? As a solemn *memento* — as a loud and awful warning to a community where justice has slumbered — and slumbered — and slumbered — while the wife has been robbed of her partner, the mother of her hopes, and life after life rashly, and with an air of triumph, sported away.

AND was there, O my GOD! no other sacrifice valuable enough — would the cry of no other blood reach the place of retribution and wake justice, dozing over her awful seat!

BUT though justice should still slumber and retribution be delayed, we who are the ministers of that GOD who will judge the judges of the world, and whose malediction rests on him who does his work unfaithfully, we will not keep silence.

I FEEL, my brethren, how incongruous my subject is with the place I occupy.

IT is humiliating; it is distressing in a Christian country, and in churches consecrated to the religion of JESUS, to be obliged to attack a crime which outstrips barbarism, and would even sink the character of a generous savage. But humiliating as it is, it is necessary.

AND must we then, even for a moment, forget the elevation on which grace hath placed us, and the light which the gospel sheds around us? Must we place ourselves back in the midst of barbarism? And instead of hearers softened to forgiveness by the love of JESUS; filled with noble sentiments towards our enemies, and waiting for occasions, after the example of Divinity, to do them good — instead of such hearers, must we suppose ourselves addressing hearts petrified to goodness, incapable of mercy, and boiling with revenge? — Must we, O my God! instead of exhorting those who hear us, to go on unto perfection, adding to *virtue charity, and to charity brotherly kindness* — must we, as if surrounded by an auditory just emerging out of darkness and still cruel and ferocious, reason to convince them that revenge is improper, and that to commit deliberate murder, is sin?

YES, we must do this. Repeated violations of the law, and the sanctuary, which the guilty find in public sentiment, prove that it is necessary.

WITHDRAW therefore for a moment, ye celestial spirits — ye holy angels accustomed to hover round these ALTARS, and listen to those strains of grace which heretofore have filled this *House of God*. Other subjects occupy us. Withdraw therefore and leave us — leave us to exhort christian parents to restrain their vengeance, and at least to keep back their hands from blood — to exhort youth, nurtured in christian families, not rashly to sport with life, nor lightly to wring the widow's heart with sorrows, and fill the orphan's eye with tears.

IN accomplishing the object which is before me, it will not be expected, as it is not necessary, that I should give a history of *Duelling*. You need not be informed that it originated in a dark and barbarous age. The polished Greek knew nothing of it — The noble Roman was above it. Rome held in equal detestation the man who exposed his life unnecessarily, and him, who refused to expose it when the public good required it.* Her he-

* Sallust de bell. Catil. ix.

roes were superior to private contests. They indulged no vengeance except against the enemies of their country. Their swords were not drawn unless her honour was in danger; which honour they defended with their swords not only, but shielded with their bosoms also, and were then prodigal of their blood.

BUT though Greece and Rome knew nothing of *Duelling*, it exists. It exists among us: and it exists at once the most *rash*, the most *absurd* and *guilty* practice, that ever disgraced a Christian nation.

GUILTY — Because it is a violation of the law. What law? The Law of GOD. THOU SHALT NOT KILL. This prohibition was delivered by GOD himself, at Sinai, to the Jews. And, that it is of universal and perpetual obligation, is manifest from the nature of the crime prohibited not only, but also from the express declaration of the Christian Lawgiver, who hath recognized its justice, and added to it the sanctions of his own authority.

"THOU shalt not kill." Who? Thou, creature. I the Creator, have given life, and thou shalt not take it away! When and under what circumstances may I not take away life? Never, and under no circumstances, without my permission. — It is obvious, that no discretion whatever is here given. The prohibition is addressed to every individual where the law of GOD is promulgated, and the terms made use of are express and unequivocal. So that life cannot be taken under any pretext, without incurring guilt, unless by a permission sanctioned by the same authority which sanctions the general law prohibiting it.

FROM this law it is granted there are exceptions.

These exceptions, however, do not result from any sovereignty which one creature has over the existence of another; but from the positive appointment of that eternal Being, whose *is the world and the fullness thereof. In whose hand is the soul of every living creature, and the breath of all mankind.*

Even the authority which we claim over the lives of animals is not founded on a natural right, but on a positive grant made by the Deity himself to Noah and his sons.* This grant contains our warrant for taking the lives of animals. But if we may not take the lives of animals without permission from God, much less may we the life of man, made in his image.

In what cases then has the Sovereign of life given this permission? In rightful war †— by the civil magistrate ‡; and in necessary self-defence.§ Besides these, I do not hesitate to declare, that in the oracles of God there are no other.

He therefore who takes life in any other case, under whatever pretext, takes it unwarrantably, is guilty of what the scriptures call murder, and exposes himself to the malediction of that God who is an avenger of blood, and who hath said, *At the hand of every man's brother will I require the life of man — Whoso sheddeth man's blood, by man shall his blood be shed.*

The duellist contravenes the law of God not only, but the law of man also. To the prohibition of the former have been added the sanctions of the latter. Life

---

* Gen. ix, 3.   † 2 Sam. x, 12. Jer. xlviii, 10.   Luke iii, 14.
‡ Ex. xxi, 12.   § Ex. xxii, 2.

taken in a duel, by the common law, is murder. And where this is not the case, the giving and receiving of a challenge only, is by statute, considered a high misdemeanor, for which the principal and his second are declared infamous, and disfranchised for twenty years.

UNDER what accumulated circumstances of aggravation does the duellist jeopardize his own life, or take the life of his antagonist?

I AM sensible that in a licentious age, and when laws are made to yield to the vices of those who move in the *higher circles*, this crime is called by I know not what mild and accommodating name. But before these altars; in this house of GOD, what is it? It is MURDER — *deliberate, aggravated*, MURDER.

IF the duellist deny this, let him produce his warrant from the Author of life, for taking away from his creature the life which had been sovereignly given. If he cannot do this, beyond all controversy, he is a murderer; for murder consists in taking away life without the permission, and contrary to the prohibition of him who gave it.

WHO is it then that calls the duellist to the dangerous and deadly combat? Is it GOD? No; on the contrary he forbids it. Is it then his country? No; she also utters her prohibitory voice. Who is it then? A man of honour. And who is this man of honour? A man perhaps whose honour is a name — who prates with polluted lips about the sacredness of character, when his own is stained with crimes, and needs but the single shade of murder to complete the dismal and sickly picture.

Every transgression of the divine law implies great guilt, because it is the transgression of infinite authority. But the crime of deliberately and lightly taking life, has peculiar aggravations. It is a crime committed against the written law not only, but also against the dictates of reason, the remonstrances of conscience, and every tender and amiable feeling of the heart.

To the unfortunate sufferer, it is the wanton violation of his most sacred rights. It snatches him from his friends and his comforts; terminates his state of trial, and precipitates him, uncalled for and perhaps unprepared, into the presence of his Judge.

You will say the duellist feels no malice. Be it so. Malice, indeed, is murder in principle. But there may be murder in reason, and in fact, where there is no malice. Some other unwarrantable passion or principle may lead to the unlawful taking of human life.

The highwayman, who cuts the throat and rifles the pocket of the passing traveller, feels no malice. And could he, with equal ease and no greater danger of detection, have secured his booty without taking life, he would have stayed his arm over the palpitating bosom of his victim, and let the plundered supplicant pass.

Would the imputation of cowardice have been inevitable to the duellist, if a challenge had not been given or accepted? The imputation of want had been no less inevitable to the robber, if the money of the passing traveller had not been secured.

Would the duellist have been willing to have spared

the life of his antagonist, if the point of honour could otherwise have been gained? So would the robber if the point of property could have been. Who can say that the motives of the one are not as urgent as the motives of the other? And the means by which both obtain the object of their wishes are the same.

THUS, according to the dictates of reason, as well as the law of GOD, the highwayman and the duellist stand on ground equally untenable; and support their guilty havoc of the human race by arguments equally fallacious.

Is duelling guilty? So it is

ABSURD. — It is absurd as a punishment, for it admits of no proportion to crimes: and besides, virtue and vice, guilt and innocence, are equally exposed by it, to death or suffering. As a reparation, it is still more absurd, for it makes the injured liable to a still greater injury. And as the vindication of personal character, it is absurd even beyond madness.

ONE man of honour, by some inadvertence, or perhaps with design, injures the sensibility of another man of honour. In perfect character the injured gentleman resents it. He challenges the offender. The offender accepts the challenge. The time is fixed. The place is agreed upon. The circumstances, with an air of solemn mania, are arranged; and the principals, with their seconds and surgeons, retire under the covert of some solitary hill, or upon the margin of some unfrequented beach, to settle this important question of honour, by stabbing or shooting at each other.

ONE or the other, or both the parties, fall in this polite and gentlemanlike contest. And what does this prove? It proves that one or the other, or both of them, as the case may be, are marksmen. But it affords no evidence that either of them possess honour, probity, or talents.

IT is true that he who falls in single combat, has the honour of being murdered: and he who takes his life, the honour of a murderer. Besides this, I know not of any glory which can redound to the infatuated combatants, except it be what results from having extended the circle of wretched widows, and added to the number of hapless orphans.

AND yet, terminate as it will, this frantic meeting, by a kind of magic influence, entirely varnishes over a defective and smutty character; transforms vice to virtue, cowardice to courage; makes falsehood truth; guilt, innocence. — In one word, it gives a new complexion to the whole state of things. The Ethiopian changes his skin, the leopard his spot, and the debauched and treacherous — having shot away the infamy of a sorry life, comes back from the field of *perfectibility* quite regenerated, and, in the fullest sense, an honourable man. He is now fit for the company of gentlemen. He is admitted to that company, and should he again by acts of vileness stain this purity of character so nobly acquired, and should any one have the affrontery to say he has done so, again he stands ready to vindicate his honour, and by another act of homicide, to wipe away the stain which has been attached to it.

I MIGHT illustrate this article by example. I might

produce instances of this mysterious transformation of character, in the sublime circles of moral refinement, furnished by the higher orders of the fashionable world, which the mere firing of pistols has produced.

But the occasion is too awful for irony.

Absurd as duelling is, were it absurd only, though we might smile at the weakness and pity the folly of its abettors, there would be no occasion for seriously attacking them — But to what has been said, I add, that duelling is *rash and presumptuous*.

Life is the gift of God, and it was never bestowed to be sported with. To each the Sovereign of the universe has marked out a sphere to move in, and assigned a part to act. This part respects ourselves not only, but others also. — Each lives for the benefit of all.

As in the system of nature the sun shines, not to display its own brightness and answer its own convenience, but to warm, enlighten, and bless the world; so in the system of animated beings, there is a dependence, a correspondence, and a relation, through an infinitely extended, dying and reviving universe — *in which no man liveth to himself, and no man dieth to himself*. Friend is related to friend; the father to his family; the individual to community. To every member of which, having fixed his station and assigned his duty, the God of nature says, " Keep this trust — defend this post." For whom? For thy friends — thy family — thy country. And having received such a charge, and for such a purpose, to desert it is rashness and temerity.

SINCE the opinions of men are as they are, do you ask, how you shall avoid the imputation of cowardice, if you do not fight when you are injured? Ask your family how you will avoid the imputation of cruelty—ask your conscience how you will avoid the imputation of guilt—ask GOD how you will avoid his malediction, if you do? These are previous questions. Let these first be answered, and it will be easy to reply to any which may follow them.

IF you only accept a challenge when you believe in your conscience that duelling is wrong, you act the coward. The dastardly fear of the world governs you. Awed by its menaces, you conceal your sentiments, appear in disguise, and act in guilty conformity to principles not your own, and that too in the most solemn moment, and when engaged in an act which exposes you to death.

BUT if it be rashness to accept, how passing rashness is it, in a sinner, to give a challenge? Does it become *him*, whose life is measured out by crimes, to be extreme to mark, and punctilious to resent, whatever is amiss in others? Must the duellist, who now disdaining to forgive, so imperiously demands satisfaction to the uttermost—must this man himself, trembling at the recollection of his offences, presently appear a suppliant before the mercy seat of GOD? Imagine this, and the case is not imaginary, and you cannot conceive an instance of greater inconsistency, or of more presumptuous arrogance. Wherefore, *avenge not yourselves, but rather give place unto wrath; for vengeance is mine, I will repay it, saith the* LORD.

Do you ask, then, how you shall conduct towards

your enemy who hath lightly done you wrong? If he be hungry, feed him; if naked, clothe him; if thirsty, give him drink. Such, had you preferred your question to *Jesus Christ*, is the answer he had given you. By observing which, you will usually subdue, and always act more honourably than your enemy.

I FEEL, my brethren, as a minister of JESUS and a teacher of his gospel, a noble elevation on this article.

COMPARE the conduct of the Christian, acting in conformity to the principles of religion, and of the duellist, acting in conformity to the principles of honour, and let reason say which bears the marks of the most exalted greatness. Compare them, and let reason say which enjoys the most calm serenity of mind in time, and which is likely to receive the plaudit of his Judge in immortality.

GOD, from his throne, beholds not a nobler object on his footstool, than the man who loves his enemies, pities their errors, and forgives the injuries they do him. This is indeed the very spirit of the heavens. It is the image of *his* benignity, whose glory fills them.

To return to the subject before us — *Guilty, absurd* and *rash*, as duelling is, it has its advocates. And had it not had its advocates — had not a strange preponderance of opinion been in favour of it, never, O lamentable *Hamilton!* hadst thou thus fallen, in the midst of thy days, and before thou hadst reached the zenith of thy glory!

O THAT I possessed the talent of eulogy, and that I

might be permitted to indulge the tenderness of friendship in paying the last tribute to his memory! O that I were capable of placing this great man before you! Could I do this, I should furnish you with an argument, the most practical, the most plain, the most convincing, except that drawn from the mandate of GOD, that was ever furnished against duelling, that horrid practice, which has in an awful moment, robbed the world of such exalted worth.

BUT I cannot do this — I can only hint at the variety and exuberance of his excellence.

THE MAN, on whom nature seems originally to have impressed the stamp of greatness — whose genius beamed from the retirement of collegiate life, with a radiance which dazzled, and a loveliness which charmed the eye of sages.

THE HERO, called from his sequestered retreat, whose first appearance in the field, though a stripling, conciliated the esteem of *Washington*, our good old father. Moving by whose side, during all the perils of the revolution, our young Chieftain was a contributer to the veteran's glory, the guardian of his person, and the compartner of his toils.

THE CONQUEROR, who, sparing of human blood, when victory favoured, stayed the uplifted arm, and nobly said to the vanquished enemy, "*LIVE!*"

THE STATESMAN, the correctness of whose principles, and the strength of whose mind, are inscribed on the records of congress, and on the annals of the council chamber; whose genius impressed itself upon the *Constitution* of his country; and whose memory, the government, *illustrious fabric*, resting on this basis, will perpetuate while it lasts: and shaken by the violence of party, should it fall, which may heaven avert, his prophetic declarations will be found inscribed on its ruins.

THE COUNSELLOR, who was at once the pride of the bar and the admiration of the court — whose apprehensions were quick as lightning, and whose developement of truth was luminous as its path — whose argument no change of circumstances could embarrass — whose knowledge appeared intuitive; and who by a single glance, and with as much facility as the eye of the eagle passes over the landscape, surveyed the whole field of controversy — saw in what way truth might be most successfully defended, and how error must be approached. And who, without ever stopping, ever hesitating, by a rapid and manly march, led the listening judge and the fascinated juror, step by step, through a delightsome region, brightening as he advanced, till his argument rose to demonstration, and eloquence was rendered useless by conviction.

WHOSE talents were employed on the side of righteousness — whose voice, whether in the council-chamber, or at the bar of justice, was virtue's consolation — At whose approach oppressed humanity felt a secret rapture, and the heart of injured innocence leapt for joy.

WHERE *Hamilton* was — in whatever sphere he moved, the friendless had a friend, the fatherless a father, and the poor man, though unable to reward his kindness, found an advocate. It was when the rich oppressed the poor — when the powerful menaced the defenceless — when truth was disregarded, or the eternal principles of justice violated — it was on these occasions, that he exerted all his strength — it was on these occasions that he sometimes soared so high and shone with a radiance so transcendant, I had almost said, so " heavenly, as filled those around him with awe, and gave to him the force and authority of a prophet."

The PATRIOT, whose integrity baffled the scrutiny of inquisition — whose manly virtue never shaped itself to circumstances — who, always great, always himself, stood amidst the varying tides of party, *firm*, like the rock, which, far from land, lifts its majestic top above the waves, and remains unshaken by the storms which agitate the ocean.

The FRIEND, who knew no guile — whose bosom was transparent and deep; in the bottom of whose heart was rooted every tender and sympathetic virtue — whose various worth opposing parties acknowledged while alive, and on whose tomb they unite, with equal sympathy and grief, to heap their honours.

I know he had his failings. I see on the picture of his life, a picture rendered awful by greatness, and luminous by virtue, some dark shades. . . . On these let the tear that pities human weakness fall : on these let the veil which covers human frailty rest. . . . As a hero, as a statesman, as a patriot, he lived nobly : and would to God I could add, he nobly fell.

Unwilling to admit his error in this respect, I go back to the period of discussion. I see him resisting the threatened interview. I imagine myself present in his chamber. Various reasons, for a time, seem to hold his determination in arrest. Various and moving objects pass before him, and speak a dissuasive language.

His country, which may need his counsels to guide, and his arm to defend, utters her *veto*. The partner of his youth, already covered with weeds, and whose tears flow down into her bosom, intercedes! His babes, stretching out their little hands and pointing to a weeping mother, with lisping eloquence, but eloquence which reaches a parent's heart, cry out " Stay — stay — dear papa, and live for us ! " In the mean time the spectre of a fallen son, pale and ghastly, approaches, opens his bleeding bosom, and as the harbinger of death, points to the yawning tomb, and warns a hesitating father of the issue !

He pauses. Reviews these sad objects : and reasons on the subject. I admire his magnanimity. I approve his reasoning, and I wait to hear him reject with indignation the murderous proposition, and to see him spurn from his presence the presumptuous bearer of it.

But I wait in vain. It was a moment in which his great wisdom forsook him. A moment in which *Hamilton* was not himself.

He yielded to the force of an imperious custom : And yielding, he sacrificed a life in which all had an interest — and he is lost — lost to his country — lost to his family — lost to us.

For this . . . . act, because he disclaimed it,

and was penitent, I forgive him. But there are those whom I cannot forgive.

I MEAN not his antagonist; over whose erring steps, if there be tears in heaven, a pious mother looks down and weeps. If he be capable of feeling, he suffers already all that humanity can suffer: Suffers, and wherever he may fly, will suffer, with the poignant recollection of having taken the life of one who was too magnanimous in return to attempt his own. Had he have known this, it must have paralyzed his arm, while it pointed, at so incorruptible a bosom, the instrument of death. Does he know this now? his heart, if it be not adamant, must soften — if it be not ice, it must melt. . . . . But on this article I forbear. Stained with blood as he is, if he be penitent, I forgive him — and if he be not, before these altars, where all of us appear as suppliants, I wish not to excite your vengeance, but rather, in behalf of an object rendered wretched and pitiable by crime, to wake your prayers.

BUT I have said, and I repeat it, there are those whom I cannot forgive.

I CANNOT forgive that minister at the altar, who has hitherto forborn to remonstrate on this subject. I cannot forgive that public prosecutor, who, intrusted with the duty of avenging his country's wrongs, has seen those wrongs, and taken no measures to avenge them. I cannot forgive that judge upon the bench, or that governor in the chair of state, who has lightly passed over such offences. I cannot forgive the public, in whose opinion the duellist finds a sanctuary. I cannot forgive you, my brethren, who, till this late hour, have been silent, while successive murders were committed. No; I cannot forgive you, that you have not, in common with the freemen of this state, raised your voice to the *powers that be*, and loudly and explicitly demanded an execution of your laws. Demanded this in a manner, which if it did not reach the ear of government, would at least have reached the heavens, and plead your excuse before the GOD that filleth them — in whose presence as I stand, I should not feel myself innocent of the blood that crieth against us, had I been silent. But I have not been silent. Many of you who hear me, are my witnesses — the walls of yonder temple, where I have heretofore addressed you, are my witnesses, how freely I have animadverted on this subject, in the presence both of those who have violated the laws, and of those whose indispensable duty it is to see the laws executed on those who violate them.

I ENJOY another opportunity; and would to GOD, I might be permitted to approach for once the late scene of death. Would to GOD, I could there assemble on the one side, the disconsolate mother with her seven fatherless children — and on the other, those who administer the justice of my country. Could I do this, I would point them to these sad objects. I would entreat them, by the agonies of bereaved fondness, to listen to the widow's heartfelt groans; to mark the orphans' sighs and tears. — And having done this, I would uncover the breathless corpse of *Hamilton* — I would lift from his gaping wound, his bloody *mantle* — I would hold it up to heaven before them, and I would ask, in the name of GOD, I would ask, whether at the sight of *it* they felt no compunction?

You will ask, perhaps, what can be done, to arrest the progress of a practice which has yet so many advocates? I answer, *nothing* — if it be the deliberate intention to do *nothing*. But if otherwise, much is within our power.

LET, then, the governor see that the laws are executed; let the council displace the man who offends against their majesty; let courts of justice frown from their bar, as unworthy to appear before them, the murderer and his accomplices; let the people declare him unworthy of their confidence who engages in such sanguinary contests; — let this be done, and should life still be taken in single combat, then the governor, the council, the court, the people, looking up to the Avenger of sin, may say, "we are innocent — we are innocent."

Do you ask how proof can be obtained? How can it be avoided? — The parties return, hold up before our eyes the instruments of death, publish to the world the circumstances of their interview, and even, with an air of insulting triumph, boast how coolly, and deliberately they proceeded in violating one of the most sacred laws of earth and heaven!

AH! ye tragic shores of Hoboken, crimsoned with the richest blood, I tremble at the crimes you record against us — the annual register of murders which you keep and send up to GOD! Place of inhuman cruelty! beyond the limits of reason, of duty, and of religion, where man assumes a more barbarous nature, and ceases to be man. What poignant, lingering sorrows do thy lawless combats occasion to surviving relatives!

YE who have hearts of pity — ye who have experienced the anguish of dissolving friendship — who have wept, and still weep over the mouldering ruins of departed kindred, ye can enter into this reflection.

O THOU disconsolate widow! robbed, so cruelly robbed, and in so short a time, both of a husband and a son, what must be the plenitude of thy sufferings! Could we approach thee, gladly would we drop the tear of sympathy, and pour into thy bleeding bosom the balm of consolation! But how could we comfort her whom GOD hath not comforted? To his throne, let us lift up our voice and weep. O GOD! if thou art still the widow's husband, and the father of the fatherless — if in the fulness of thy goodness there be yet mercies in store for miserable mortals, pity, O pity this afflicted mother, and grant that her hapless orphans may find a friend, a benefactor, a father, in THEE!

ON this article I have done: and may GOD add his blessing.

BUT I have still a claim upon your patience. I cannot here repress my feelings, and thus let pass the present opportunity. . . .

How are the mighty fallen! And, regardless as we are of vulgar deaths, shall not the fall of the *mighty* affect us?

A SHORT time since, and he who is the occasion of our sorrows, was the ornament of his country. He stood on an eminence; and glory covered him. From that eminence he has fallen — suddenly, forever, fallen. His intercourse with the living world is now ended; and those who would hereafter find him, must seek him in the grave. There, cold and lifeless, is the heart which just now was the seat of friendship. There, dim and sightless, is the eye, whose radiant and enlivening orb beamed with intelligence; and there, closed for ever, are those lips, on whose persuasive accents we have so often, and so lately, hung with transport!

From the darkness which rests upon his tomb, there proceeds, methinks, a light in which it is clearly seen that those gaudy objects which men pursue, are only phantoms. In this light how dimly shines the splendour of victory — how humble appears the majesty of grandeur! The bubble which seemed to have so much solidity, has burst; and we again see that all below the sun is vanity. . . .

True, the funeral eulogy has been pronounced; the sad and solemn procession has moved; the badge of mourning has already been decreed, and presently the sculptured marble will lift up its front, proud to perpetuate the name of HAMILTON, and rehearse to the passing traveller his virtues.

Just tributes of respect! And to the living useful. But to him, mouldering in his narrow and humble habitation, what are they? — How vain! how unavailing!

Approach, and behold — while I lift from his sepulchre its covering! — Ye admirers of his greatness; ye emulous of his talents and his fame, approach, and behold him now. How pale! — How silent! — No martial bands admire the adroitness of his movements: No fascinated throng weep — and melt — and tremble, at his eloquence!— Amazing change! A shroud! a coffin! a narrow, subterraneous cabin! This is all that now remains of *Hamilton*! And is this all that remains of *him*? — During a life so transitory, what lasting monument then can our fondest hopes erect?

MY brethren! we stand on the borders of an *awful gulf*, which is swallowing up all things human. And is there, amidst this universal wreck, nothing stable, nothing abiding, nothing immortal, on which poor, frail, dying man, can fasten?

ASK the hero, ask the statesman, whose wisdom you have been accustomed to revere, and he will tell you. He will tell you, did I say? He has already told you, from his death-bed, and his illumined spirit still whispers from the heavens, with well known eloquence, the solemn admonition:

"MORTALS! hastening to the tomb, and once the companions of my pilgrimage, take warning and avoid my errors — Cultivate the virtues I have recommended — Choose the Saviour I have chosen — Live disinterestedly — Live for immortality; and would you rescue any thing from final dissolution, lay it up in GOD."

THUS speaks, methinks, our deceased benefactor, and thus he acted during his last sad hours. To the exclusion of every other concern, *religion* now claims all his thoughts.

JESUS! JESUS, is now his only hope. The friends of JESUS are his friends — the ministers of the altar his companions. While these intercede, he listens in awful silence, or in profound submission whispers his assent.

SENSIBLE, deeply sensible of his sins, he pleads no merit of his own. He repairs to the mercy seat, and there pours out his penitential sorrows — there he solicits pardon.

HEAVEN, it should seem, heard and pitied the suppliant's cries. Disburdened of his sorrows, and looking up to GOD, he exclaims, " Grace — rich grace." "I have," said he, clasping his dying hands, and with a faltering tongue, " *I have a tender reliance on the mercy of God in Christ.*" In token of this reliance, and as an expression of his faith, he receives the holy sacrament; and having done this, his mind becomes tranquil and serene. Thus he remains, thoughtful indeed, but unruffled to the last, and meets death with an air of dignified composure, and with an eye directed to the heavens.

THIS last act, more than any other, sheds glory on his character. Every thing else death effaces. Religion alone abides with him on his death-bed. He dies a Christian. This is all which can be enrolled of him among the archives of eternity. This is all that can make his name great in heaven.

LET not the sneering infidel persuade you that this last act of homage to the Saviour, resulted from an enfeebled state of mental faculties, or from perturbation occasioned by the near approach of death. No; his opinions concerning the Divine Mission of *Jesus Christ*, and the validity of the holy scriptures, had long been settled, and settled after laborious investigation and extensive and deep research. These opinions were not concealed. I knew them myself. Some of you who hear me, knew them; and had his life been spared, it was his determination to have published them to the world, together with the facts and reasons on which they were founded.

At a time when scepticism, shallow and superficial indeed, but depraved and malignant, is breathing forth its pestilential vapour, and polluting by its unhallowed touch, every thing divine and sacred; it is consoling to a devout mind to reflect, that the great, and the wise, and the good of all ages; those superior geniuses, whose splendid talents have elevated them almost above mortality, and placed them next in order to angelic natures — Yes, it is consoling to a devout mind to reflect, that while *dwarfish infidelity* lifts up its deformed head, and mocks, these *illustrious personages*, though living in different ages — inhabiting different countries — nurtured in different schools — destined to different pursuits — and differing on various subjects — should all, as if touched with an impulse from heaven, agree to vindicate the sacredness of Revelation, and present with one accord, their learning, their talents and their virtue, on the Gospel Altar, as an offering to Emanuel.

This is not exaggeration. Who was it, that, overleaping the narrow bounds which had hitherto been set to the human mind, ranged abroad through the immensity of space, discovered and illustrated those laws by which the *Deity* unites, binds, and governs all things? Who was it, soaring into the sublime of astronomic science, numbered the stars of heaven, measured their spheres, and called them by their names? It was Newton. But Newton was a Christian. Newton, great as he was, received instruction from the lips, and laid his honours at the feet of *Jesus*.

Who was it, that developed the hidden combination, the component parts of bodies? Who was it, dissected the animal, examined the flower, penetrated the earth, and ranged the extent of organic nature? It was BOYLE. But Boyle was a Christian.

Who was it, that lifted the veil which had for ages covered the intellectual world, analyzed the human mind, defined its powers, and reduced its operations to certain and fixed laws? It was LOCKE. But Locke too was a Christian.

What more shall I say? For time would fail me, to speak of *Hale*, learned in the law; of *Addison*, admired in the schools; of *Milton*, celebrated among the poets; and of *Washington*, immortal in the field and the cabinet. — To this catalogue of professing Christians, from among, if I may speak so, a higher order of beings, may now be added the name of ALEXANDER HAMILTON — A name which raises in the mind the idea of whatever is great, whatever is splendid, whatever is illustrious in human nature; and which is now added to a catalogue which might be lengthened — and lengthened — and lengthened, with the names of illustrious characters, whose lives have blessed society, and whose works form a COLUMN high as heaven — a column of learning, of wisdom, and of greatness, which will stand to future ages, an *eternal monument* of the transcendant talents of the advocates of Christianity, when every fugitive leaf, from the pen of the canting infidel witlings of the day, shall be swept by the tide of time from the annals of the world, and buried with the names of their authors in oblivion.

To conclude. *How are the mighty fallen!* Fallen before the desolating hand of death. Alas! the ruins of the tomb. . . . . The ruins of the tomb are an emblem of the ruins of the world. When not an individual, but an universe, already marred by sin and hastening to dissolution, shall agonize and die! Directing your thoughts from the one, fix them for a moment on the other. Anticipate the concluding scene, the final catastrophe of nature: when the sign of the Son of man shall be seen in heaven; when the son of man himself shall appear in the glory of his Father, and send forth judgment unto victory — The fiery desolation envelopes towns, palaces, and fortresses; the heavens pass away! The earth melts! and all those magnificent productions of art, which ages, heaped on ages, have reared up, are in one awful day reduced to ashes!

AGAINST the ruins of that day, as well as the ruins of the tomb which precede it, the gospel, in the *cross* of its great *High Priest*, offers you all a sanctuary; a sanctuary secure and abiding; a sanctuary, which no lapse of time, nor change of circumstances, can destroy. No; neither life nor death — No; neither principalities nor powers.

EVERY thing else is fugitive; every thing else is mutable; every thing else will fail you. But this, the *citadel* of the Christian's hopes, will never fail you. Its base is adamant. It is cemented with the richest blood. The ransomed of the Lord crowd its portals. Enbosomed in the dust which it incloses, the bodies of the redeemed "rest in hope." On its top dwells the Church of the first born, who in delightful response with the angels of light, chant redeeming love. Against this Citadel the tempest beats, and around it the storm rages, and spends its force in vain. Immortal in its nature, and incapable of change, it stands, and stands firm, amidst the ruins of a mouldering world, and endures forever.

THITHER fly, ye prisoners of hope!—that when earth, air, elements, shall have passed away, secure of existence and felicity, you may join with saints in glory, to perpetuate the song which lingered on the faultering tongue of HAMILTON, "*Grace — rich Grace.*"

GOD grant us this honour: Then shall the measure of our joy be full, and to his name shall be the glory in *Christ.* — AMEN.

Extract of a letter from a respectable gentleman in Virginia, dated 16*th July.*

"WITHIN a day or two past a report has pervaded this part of the country, of the death of Gen. Hamilton, in a duel with Col. Burr. The report, it is said, is too well authenticated to be doubted, though as yet, I am uninformed of the particulars. — Alas! and was this to be the fate of a man, who would have been an honour to any country upon earth? Execrated be the custom in general, and execrated be the hand in particular, that could aim the means of death, under sanction of this custom, at one, who when he fell, left not his equal, take him all in all, upon the surface of our globe. Alas! Illustrious shade, farewell! Our country's loss in you is irreparable. Your name, and well known worth and talents, operated strongly in favour to our country, even upon the ambitious designs of him, who grasps in imagination, the empire of the world. He knew that *your* sagacity and vigilance could not be deceived, and that in times of difficulty and danger, when they should be apparent, *you*, like Washington, would become the bulwark of our safety — that all true American hearts in such a crisis, forgetting their former resentments and delusions, would be united. But now whither are we to turn in such an event? Execrated be the hand that has robbed our country of this transcendant worth! But, alas! it can never be recalled!"

THE two letters from which the following extracts are now made, were received soon after their respective dates. They have not been printed before, because, as they were not designed for the public eye, they contained some passages which I thought had better be suppressed; but they are so eloquently written that I cannot refuse myself the satisfaction of presenting at least some passages from them.

Extract of a letter from a gentleman in Burlington, (N. J.) dated July 16, 1804.

"No country ever deplored a greater man, nor did ever the tears of friendship embalm a memory so pregnant with worth and honour. Alas! how unavailing is all that admiration and gratitude, which, too late, would fain reanimate him from the grave! . . . .

"His life has long been sought for, as the last sacrifice to malignant and criminal passions; yet, even in his death, he presents an image of sublime heroism and virtue, terrifying to guilty minds. What, indeed, must be the overwhelming brightness of that character, which forces the very assassins of his reputation and life, to retract their calumnies, and wear the ensigns of mourning! This event removes out of the way, perhaps, the only remaining obstacle to the domineering projects of Virginia. *Two* men only, lived in this degenerate country, whose opinions and energy retarded the march of cunning ambition — They are *gone* — fortunate, perhaps, after lives of patriotism and unceasing usefulness, not quite to have out-lived the liberties of their country. I much regret that it never fell to my lot to have even seen this truly wonderful man: his qualities were such, however, as to attract the warmest personal attachments. — What *American*, but in his admiration of the Hero and Statesman, will mingle sighs for *Hamilton* himself? — but then, pleasing consolation!

> ——— He's gone to Virtue's rest!
> "With all his country's wishes blest.
> When Spring, with dewy fingers cold,
> Returns to deck his hallowed mould;
> She there shall dress a sweeter sod
> Than Fancy's feet have ever trod.
> By fairy hands his knell is rung;
> By forms unseen his dirge is sung;
> There *Honour* comes, a pilgrim grey,
> To bless the turf that wraps his clay;
> And *Freedom* shall awhile repair,
> To dwell a weeping Hermit there.
>   COLLINS.

"I CAN only add, that here, (as I suppose every where else) grief clouds every countenance."

Extract of another from the same, dated July 20.

"I CANNOT disburthen my heart enough to be submissive to this punishment of God upon an ungrateful land: He that ought to have been the pride and favourite of his country, as he was its soul and saviour; was first smitten with the death of ingratitude, and then butchered by one of your . . . I am impatient and feverish with the subject. Adieu."

TRIBUTE OF RESPECT.

At a special Meeting of the St. Andrew's Society of the City of Albany, held at the Tontine Coffee-House, July 26th, 1804:

Resolved unanimously, That in token of the sincere grief of the Society for the premature and untimely death of General Alexander Hamilton, and the high sense they entertain of his distinguished services to his country, as a Soldier and a Statesman; of the eminent virtues which adorned him as a man, a friend, and a citizen, and the high respect in which he has justly been held by our Sister Society of the City of New-York, of which he was one of its first members; that they, at every meeting of the Society for six months, shall appear with an appropriate badge of mourning.

Resolved, That the Rev. John M'Donald, Mr. Pearson, Mr. Ramsay, and Dr. M'Clelland, be a committee to prepare a respectful message of condolence to General Philip Schuyler, the venerable and afflicted father-in-law of our dear deceased brother, expressive of the sympathy of this Society with him and his family, in their irreparable loss, and that they convey the same in the most delicate manner to the General.

GENERAL PHILIP SCHUYLER.

Sir,

THE President and Members of the *St. Andrew's Society* of the City of Albany, beg leave with mingled sensations of grief and indignation, to tender you their sincere and respectful condolence on the untimely death of Alexander Hamilton, a distinguished son of your family, an early member of the *American St. Andrew Societies*, and the ornament and pride of the American people.

YOU, Sir, have been long acquainted with his singular merits, and with the amiable qualities of his heart. You have never ceased, with candour and generosity, to appreciate and respect them. But he has fallen, cruelly fallen, at a time when your age and infirmities rendered his correspondence and occasional society peculiarly desirable and soothing; and at a time when his excellent wife and his rising family, in various views, demanded his protection, his counsel, and exertion; at a time when the situation of our country seems to require his vigilance and his warning. He has fallen by the hand of a man, whom his gentle and generous nature could only injure by eclipsing him, or by conscientiously attempting to counteract or defeat measures which he deemed dangerous to the community. His fall, though premature, will seal his own unspotted fame, and an odium on his implacable opponent, which time will not remove.

THE fame of Hamilton will need no protecting shield, though thousands, were it necessary, would rejoice in the office: It will continue to spread with increasing glory beyond the limits, and probably beyond the duration of the government which he eminently contributed to establish.

Could this Society, could our country in general, devise means for mitigating the grief of a brave soldier, of a faithful and indefatigable statesman, under your present unexpected and heavy calamity, they would not be withheld. But in the bosom of an honourable and independent retirement, surrounded with a flourishing and affectionate family, and blessed with the resources of an active, capacious, and cultivated mind, we trust you will be enabled to support with dignity, what you can never cease to deplore.

May propitious Heaven shed peculiar rays of comfort on an useful and laborious life, qualify you for the protection and consolation of the afflicted relatives of the honourable dead, and grant you a late, but joyful admission to the abodes of peace, and the society of the good.

Signed by order, and in behalf of the Society, at a Special Meeting, the 26th July, 1804.

JOHN M'DONALD,
GEORGE RAMSAY,
GEORGE PEARSON,
WM. M'CLELLAND,
Committee.

Albany, *July* 27.
Gentlemen,

My warmest and unfeigned acknowledgments are due to the President, and the members of the St. Andrew's

Society, for the delicate and feeling manner in which they have condoled with me, on the irreparable loss I have sustained in the death of a son, who had endeared himself to me by the most tender solicitude: who was the kindest and most affectionate husband to my dear and distressed daughter: who, as a father, unremittingly inculcated into the tender minds of his children, that virtue which marked his life, and that love of their creator whom he adored.

UNDER the pressure of so severe a calamity, the honour paid by the Society to the memory of the deceased, the humane attempt to console and mitigate the heart-rending distress of an aged and feeble parent, are not only soothing, but will, with resignation to the divine dispensation, impart a ray of comfort to my wounded bosom.

PERMIT me, Gentlemen, through you, to reciprocate with the utmost cordiality, those affectionate wishes which have evidently emanated from the hearts of the Society, and which it has pleased them so strongly to express for me and my family — And do you, gentlemen, be pleased to accept of my best acknowledgments for the marked and polite manner in which you have conveyed the sense of the Society, on this mournful event.

I am, Gentlemen, very respectfully,
Your obliged and obedient servant,
PH: SCHUYLER.

To the Rev. John M'Donald, Messrs. Ramsay, Pearson, and M'Clelland.

THE UTICA PATRIOT.

At a numerous and respectable meeting of the inhabitants of Whitestown and the vicinity, holden at the Hotel in Utica, on the 24th of July, 1804, the following resolutions were unanimously adopted:

This Meeting having heard, with inexpressible sorrow, of the death of Gen. Hamilton, and being desirous of paying a tribute of respect to the rare union of great virtues and transcendent talents, which have exalted and adorned his character; and believing that in the death of this great and good man, our country has lost one of its great benefactors, and the world one of its brightest ornaments:

Resolved Unanimously, That it be recommended to the inhabitants of Whitestown and its vicinity, to set apart Thursday the 26th inst. as a day of public mourning, for this melancholy and important event; and that there be a general suspension of business on that day:

That minute guns be fired during the morning, under the direction of Capt. Kirkland, of the Artillery:

And, that Mr. J. H. Lothrop be requested to deliver an Address suited to the occasion, at 12 o'clock on that day, at the new Church in Whitesborough, where our fellow-citizens are requested to attend.

Resolved, That Mr. Jonas Platt, Mr. J. Van Rensselaer, and Mr. Gerrit G. Lansing, be a committee to carry the foregoing resolutions into effect.

Resolved, That it be recommended to our fellow-citizens of Whitestown, to wear crape on the left arm as mourning, during thirty days.

Resolved, That the proceedings of this meeting, signed by the chairman and secretary, be published in the next Patriot and Columbian Gazette.

>B. WALKER, *Chairman.*
>T. SKINNER, *Secretary.*

>*Whitesborough, Thursday, July* 26.

In pursuance of the foregoing resolutions, all business being suspended, minute guns were fired during the morning from an adjacent eminence; and the tolling of the village bell announced the death of our beloved HAMILTON.

At 12 o'clock great numbers of all classes of citizens assembled, and a procession was formed in the following order, viz.

>Sheriff Brodhead and his Deputies,
>Citizens,
>Physicians,
>Students of law,
>Gentlemen of the Bar,
>Magistrates,
>Orator,
>Committee of Arrangement.

The procession then moved in solemn silence to the new Church, where an elegant and appropriate Address was delivered by *John H. Lothrop,* Esq. to a large and afflicted audience.

The public expressions of sorrow and respect every where exhibited, show that the character of HAMILTON is *now* appreciated as it deserves: Posterity, we know, will take care of his fame.

A CITIZEN.

THE RECORDER OF THE TIMES. (*Democratic.*)

Hamilton is no more!—A main pillar of the state has fallen; not by the giant arm of a Samson, but by the persevering malice of the ruthless, the weak, and intriguing Saul.—The most distant parts of our country have felt the shock.

Hamilton was virtuous, eloquent, and brave. Envy herself drooped at the lustre of his virtues; his opponents were melted by his eloquence, and his enemies confounded by his bravery. In justice he was an Aristides; in eloquence a Cicero, and an Achilles in war. An opportunity would have enabled him to have astonished the world, by the splendour of his military achievements. But he has been snatched from his country in the prime of life, and has left us nothing but the remembrance of his greatness. The day which terminated *his* career, annihilated a star of the first magnitude.

GENERAL HAMILTON.

"The Corporation and Citizens of Burlington, New-Jersey, are respectfully invited to attend at the Town-House, to-morrow evening, at 7 o'clock, for the purpose of uniting in some public expression of their respect for the memory of General Hamilton.

James Sterling, Mayor.

Friday, 20th July, 1804.

IN pursuance of this request, the citizens having assembled, appointed the Mayor, Chairman, and Mr. M'Ilvaine, the Recorder, Secretary.

MR. GRIFFITH introduced the melancholy subject in these terms:—

A LIFE which was only devoted to *Honour* and its *Country*, is no longer ours.

IN the meridian of his days — of his usefulness — and of his fame — *Hamilton* has descended to the tomb!

WHO can look back, upon the public services, and exalted virtues of the deceased, without exclaiming in the anguish of despair — '*Is he*, too, numbered among the silent dead?'

YES, the *martial son* of Washington, who shared with him the toils and dangers of a war for *liberty*, (O pious hope!) is united to him in the realms of eternal peace.

THAT luminous and expanded *mind*, which embraced all knowledge, and was applied to the utmost good of his fellow-men — is fled to the *spirit* which gave it.

THOSE pure and tender *affections*, which imparted to social intercourse all that could attract and delight, have disappeared.

THAT *eloquence*, on which a listening Senate hung, is for ever silent. Yet these shall never be forgotten.

HIS *memory* will only cease to inspire and to charm,

when *Americans* cease to honour and love the courage which achieved their independence, and the wisdom which cemented their Union.

We are assembled for the generous purpose of uniting in the performance of some feeble expression of our gratitude, our admiration, and our grief. Alas! in our *hearts* only must be sought the real extent of those feelings; I forbear to speak; it is enough now to *weep* over the man, whom History, his Country, and the World, shall delight to rank among the Constellations of Genius, Virtue, and Valour."

The following resolution was immediately adopted:—

"At an Assembly of the Citizens of Burlington, in the Town-House, on Saturday the 21st of July, 1804— it was unanimously agreed thus publicly to express the deep affliction which the premature death of General Alexander Hamilton imparts to every bosom; to acknowledge the debt of gratitude, which was due to him for a continued series of inestimable services in war and peace; to avow a conscious pride in the character of an American Citizen, who lived to defend, to bless, and to adorn his Country; and lastly, to deplore the tyranny of that custom, which has suddenly borne away domestic peace, and left a nation in tears."

Published at the special request of the citizens:

JAMES STERLING, *Chairman.*
JOS. M'ILVAINE, *Secretary.*

END OF NO. III.

A COLLECTION, &c.

Nº. IV.

FROM A BOSTON PAPER, JULY 26.

Tribute of respect to the Memory of General ALEXANDER HAMILTON.

THIS day the Committee of Arrangement respectfully give notice, that the Eulogy on the late Gen. Alexander Hamilton, will be pronounced at the Chapel Church, at twelve o'clock.

THOSE of their fellow-citizens, who are disposed to unite in paying this public respect to the merits and illustrious services of the deceased, are requested to assemble at a quarter before twelve o'clock, on the State-House floor; and from thence accompany the Orator to the Church.

  By order, J. WARREN, *Chairman.*
Thursday, July 26, 1804.

ATTENTION!

THE Independent Cadets will assemble at Faneuil-Hall, this morning at nine o'clock, in Uniform complete, with white Gaiters. The roll will be called at half past nine precisely.

      Wm. SHIMMIN, O. S.

Arrangements at the Chapel.

The public are respectfully informed, that all the Galleries, and a part of the Wall Pews on the lower floor, in the Chapel, will be exclusively appropriated to the Ladies. — The six first Pews on the Broad Aile, will be reserved for the Military Escort, and all the remainder of the Body Pews on the lower floor, for those who compose the procession.

The forming of the procession, at a quarter before 12 o'clock, will be announced by the tolling of the Chapel bell, which will cease as soon as the procession has entered the Church. *By desire of the Committee of Arrangements,*

JOSEPH MAY.

LAST TRIBUTE OF RESPECT.

In willing conformity to the resolutions of the respectable body of citizens, who assembled on Friday Evening last, we are happy in learning that the meeting this day, at the New State-House, will be general; that no party distinctions will appear; and that our citizens, universally, will adopt the recommended *Badge of Mourning*, on the occasion. The acknowledged pre-eminent services and talents of the illustrious deceased, would have called for these marks of respect for his memory, and regret for their cessation, if the example of our cities of New-York, Philadelphia, Wilmington, Baltimore, &c. had not benignantly beckoned us to follow. Foremost in every good work, the citizens of Boston, in the grateful homage they are about to pay, will still evince to the world, that on great occasions, *they ever rise superior to party impulse;* that they will recognize and reverence merit, services, and patriotism, wherever they may be found: and that in native independence, and genuine liberality, they are not inferior in any degree, to the best citizens of any other portion of the continent. Those who loved and revered Washington, must respect the memory of him whom *Washington respected* as a *Friend*, a *Confidant*, a *Counsellor*. — Those who esteemed tried Patriotism as one of the most exalted virtues, must weep over the bier of the Patriot " *without reproach* " — and those who knew the dangers of the " *tented field*," when Independence was the stake contended for, and are not unwilling to acknowledge services which were *faithful to the end*, will not decline to strew roses over the grave of the *Soldier-Citizen*, and *Citizen-Soldier*.

The masters of such vessels as are lying at the wharves, as well as those at anchor in the harbour, will show their respect to departed merit, by hoisting their colours half mast, during the solemnities of the day.

SAME PAPER, JULY 27.
TRIBUTE TO MERIT.

Yesterday was the day assigned for public demonstration of the esteem and respect of the citizens of Boston, for the merits and illustrious services of the late Gen. Hamilton. At half past 12 o'clock a procession was formed at the State-House. It consisted of the Committee of Arrangements, Orator, Chaplain, His Honour the Lieut. Governor, Judges of the Supreme Court, foreign Consuls, Strangers of distinction, and citizens; and included near 1000 persons. The procession moved through Winter and Marlborough-streets and a part of Cornhill and Court-street, to the Chapel Church, escorted by the independent Cadets, under the command of Major Pierce. The Throne of Grace was addressed in an appropriate prayer by the Rev. Chaplain of the House of Representatives, and an Anthem suited to the occasion was sung, after which an Eulogy on the Character of the deceased Patriot and Statesman, was pronounced by the Hon. Harrison G. Otis, Esq.

The Hon. Mr. King, and Judge Benson, of New-York, and the Hon. Mr. Rutledge, of S. Carolina, were among the auditors at the Chapel yesterday.

Most of the public offices were closed; the flags of the shipping in the harbour were suspended at half-mast through the day; and during the moving of the procession, minute guns were fired from Fort Independence.

SALEM PAPER.

Yesterday were performed at Boston, the public and solemn ceremonies of respect to the memory of Gen. Hamilton. At 12 o'clock a very long procession composed of the first characters of the metropolis and the vicinity, moved from the State-House to the Chapel Church, escorted by the Independent Cadets; where, after a prayer by the Rev. Mr. Kirkland, in a very elevated strain of devotion, and an appropriate hymn, the Honourable Mr. Otis pronounced an Eulogy on the character of the deceased. Of this composition, which was delivered with the greatest effect, we can give but a faint outline. After a pathetic exordium, (in which it was observed with felicity that " the sod which was still wet with our tears for Washington, was now to be disturbed to receive the friend of Washington — the disciple that leaned upon his bosom,") Mr. Otis presented a rapid but glowing sketch of the life of General Hamilton. With this were necessarily intervolved all the great events of our national history, from the commencement of the revolution. A forcible appeal was made to the gratitude of the nation, when the audience were reminded that in addition to the many subordinate public measures of which Hamilton was the author, he first proclaimed the necessity of an amendment of the old confederation; and that the address to the people for calling a General Convention was the production of his pen. The unwearied patriotism which he displayed in promoting the adoption of the Constitution, and the immortal work written with that view, were next glanced at. The simplicity of his habits, and his scanty but honest earnings on his quitting public employments, were very happily contrasted with the rapacity and avarice of the Generals and Financiers of the French Republic. Those unprincipled plunderers were called upon to disgorge their ill-gotten wealth — to quit their gorgeous palaces, and with shame to humble themselves before the simple tomb of Hamilton. — His errors (for he was human) were also touched upon — but they were touched with the hand of a friend. — The delineation of his character was executed with the skill of a master. — Just praise, without the disgusting extravagance of flattery (but indeed what could be flattery of Hamilton?) was bestowed with a generous liberality. In short, the performance in the whole was a most honourable testimonial of the distinguished virtues and resplendent talents of the departed patriot.

This sketch (which we made from memory, and under the disadvantage of an unfavourable situation in the church) will, we are sensible, convey a very inadequate idea of the merit of the composition: But we shall the less regret it, as we trust the public will soon be gratified by the perusal of the Eulogy itself.

ALBANY GAZETTE.

IN compliance with the request of the citizens of Albany, discourses were yesterday delivered in several of the churches of this city, on the untimely and ever to be lamented death of General HAMILTON. The concourse of people in the North Church, was the most respectable and numerous ever before assembled on any occasion in this city, the death of General *Washington* only excepted: The Rev. Mr. Nott led their devotions — and in a discourse the most luminous and impressive, he contemplated, reviewed, and made an appropriate application of that sublime passage of Holy Writ: " *The Beauty of Israel is slain upon the high places: How are the mighty fallen!* "

FROM THE TRENTON FEDERALIST.

IN the early part of last week, the man who has covered our country with mourning, Col. Aaron Burr, passed through the state of Jersey, on his way to Philadelphia, where, we are informed, he has had the hardihood to make a public appearance by walking in the open streets in the face of day. From Amboy he was carried by some friend to Cranberry, and thence conveyed in a *light-waggon*, crossing the Delaware at Lamberton ferry, to Bristol, in Pennsylvania. — Stopping at a tavern a few miles beyond the Delaware, he was recognized by the honest landlord, who, unapprized of the desire of concealment, called him by his proper name. On this he requested the landlord no more to make use of his name while he staid at the house! These things we are enabled to state as unquestionably true, in consequence of the correctness of the source from which we received them. How degrading to the majesty of our government, that its second officer should thus be under the real or fancied necessity of travelling with studied privacy, through bye-roads, and in unusual vehicles! It becomes the man, however, who has extinguished the bright constellation of genius and worth, himself to walk in darkness and obscurity. — It manifests some deference to public opinion, and the energy of the laws. Whether the arm of justice would have been raised to stop him in his course, we know not. — Nor know we whether any measures will be taken to wash out the precious blood which stains the shores of Jersey. The path of duty we apprehend is plain. — It is well known by him to whom is intrusted the dignity of the state, and if we are to rely on general promises of official faithfulness, he will follow it. The honour of New-Jersey demands that its shores should no longer be made places of butchery for the inhabitants of New-York and Pennsylvania.

THE BALANCE.

[THE heart of Croswell vents its grief in the following pathetic strain :]

A Tribute. — From the editor of this paper, something more is due to the departed HAMILTON, than common panegyric and general encomium. This, a whole nation is bound to bestow — this, not a citizen of America seems disposed to withhold. But to me he once rendered unequalled service, apart from that rendered to his country generally. In my defence, and in defence of the American press, he once exerted his unrivalled eloquence. In my cause, this greatest of men made his mightiest effort — an effort, which might have palsied the up-lifted hand of power — an effort, which might have carried terror to the bosom of a tyrant. For this service, *voluntarily rendered*, I owed him a debt of gratitude which never could be cancelled — never diminished. But, by offering my feeble aid to the support of principles which he advocated, I hoped, at least, to show my sense of the obligation under which I was laid, by his disinterested exertions — Alas! he is gone — and I have only returned him the *professions* of my gratitude. But "*his fame is left*" — *dear as my blood, my life shall be devoted to its protection.*

NEW-ENGLAND REPUBLICAN.

SEVERAL editorial paragraphs, and articles of news, are omitted this week to give place to the correspondence which preceded and terminated in the death of General ALEXANDER HAMILTON. His funeral rites, performed on Saturday the 14th inst. with every possible solemnity, do much honour to the citizens of New-York. All know the cause of his death, and all will bear it in mind. Let the citizens of these States for ever remember, that his life was devoted to their service. Let them remember, that it was through anxiety for their welfare, that he gave the offence which [was the cause of] his death. He saw himself under the necessity of either permitting them to be deceived by professions which he suspected to be false; or, in cautioning them against their danger, of giving offence to their enemies. He did not hesitate for a moment. He cannot be suspected of being influenced by party animosity, nor of seeking promotion on the ruin of his adversary. He was then a private citizen, and his determination to remain so was unchanged. Seeing with concern the intrigues of men whose views he could not justify, in the frankness of his heart he uttered his fears; and for this generous indiscretion he lost his life. Yet the *cause* of his death must not be sought for here [only]; but in that pride which could not brook a superior; that envy which sickened at his fame; that ambition which maddened with impediments; that spirit of revenge which counted not the price of its gratification. The hand raised against him, was moved by a heart which never melted at his eloquence; and directed by an eye which lowered upon his excellence. Hamilton did not die by the hand of a Brutus; he commanded no power but the mild influence of his character; he headed no army but the pacific legions of his virtues. He had never subjugated his country; nor, by his approach to absolute power, invited the offer of a crown. Yet was he branded a Cæsar. His death was not the consequence of a recent offence: it had long been desired, and a pretext long sought for. When Washington invited him to his confidence; when he conferred upon him marks of his esteem as he delighted to do; the heart which moved the hand against him, sunk in envy. Alas! that private hatred should be able to deprive the world of such a mind as his; such a rare versatility of talents; such a group of mild virtues. Those who had before condemned the practice of duelling, as inconsistent with religion and the laws of the land, will now have an additional reason for their disapprobation. It has deprived his family of a husband and father; his friends of a cheerful companion; his profession of its proudest boast; society of a benevolent and active member; his country of her bravest champion, and the world of an honest man. All this mischief was the work of private revenge!

NEWPORT MERCURY.

As the public appear to be highly interested in the melancholy death of that eminently distinguished Patriot and Soldier, Gen. *Alexander Hamilton*, we have appropriated a large proportion of this day's paper to the publication of those arrangements made in New-York for his solemn interment, and for the general expression of that sorrow which appears to have pervaded all ranks and parties in the city. Want of room prevents our publishing the correspondence between Gen. Hamilton and Col. Burr, before next week, when the public shall be gratified, by a perusal of all the communications on this subject, by which it will very evidently appear, that there existed in the mind of Col. Burr, a predetermined hostility and inveteracy of design, which no language could assuage — no honourable concession could appease.

ALTHOUGH we explicitly condemn the barbarous and unchristian custom of duelling, so shamefully prevalent in our country, yet it affords us much satisfaction, under this great national calamity, to ascertain the pleasing fact . . . that Gen. Hamilton, with extreme reluctance [only], under what he honestly conceived, imperious necessity . . . was induced to wave his conscientious scruples against this unequal mode of terminating disputes; and that, such was his conduct, during the last solemn scene of his life, as to induce a belief, that he died at peace with the world, and reconciled in sacred love to his God.

> " 'T is just to give applause, where 't is deserv'd;
> His virtues, sure, have stood the test of fortune;
> Like purest gold, that, tortured in the furnace,
> Comes out more bright, and brings forth all its weight."

"How does the lustre of this great man's actions,
Through the dark cloud of ills that covered him,
Break forth, and shine with more triumphant brightness."

THE CONNECTICUT GAZETTE.

AT Philadelphia, Boston, and other places, we perceive that tributes of great respect are paid to the memory of the beloved and lamented *Hamilton*. An eulogy is to be delivered by Harrison G. Otis, Esq. at Boston, and the citizens are recommended to wear crape for thirty days. — The citizens of Philadelphia assembled and passed several resolves honorary to the deceased, predicated on the following : " That a national tribute of respect to the memory of departed heroes and statesmen, not only excites an emulation of their glorious example, but constitutes the purest reward of their toils and their virtues ; and that such a tribute is justly due to the memory of Alexander Hamilton." The bells were tolled, the colours of the vessels were displayed half-mast, and the citizens were requested to wear crape on the left arm for thirty days.

As General Hamilton, in point of national services, stood among the first of those worthies who achieved our Independence, and contributed probably more than any other man, to the adoption of our excellent constitution, his death at any time would have caused a general grief; but the premature and tragic manner in which he was torn from us, has justly excited a national feeling of sorrow and indignation, honourable to our national character, and to the memory of the deceased. The loss of so much talents and integrity at this time, is no common deprivation. Every citizen has lost a friend, and every honourable man a brother.

Consulting the sentiments and feeling of the public, we have appropriated a considerable portion of our paper to this interesting subject, and doubt not the approbation of our readers.

THE NORFOLK LEDGER.

Let us Mourn!!! — The good, the wise, the patriotic Alexander Hamilton; whose whole life was devoted to the service of man; from the exercise of whose talents, this country has derived benefits of the most incalculable magnitude: His Arm was exerted for our Independence: — His Science in framing our Constitution: — His Eloquence in obtaining its adoption: — His Knowledge in originating our Finance. And those blessings which he had so eminently contributed to obtain, he has ever shown himself the most forward to defend and insure. This great and virtuous man, who was the unchanging friend of his country, who was the invaluable friend of Washington, died, on Thursday, July 12, 1804, at the house of William Bayard, Esq. at Greenwich, in consequence of a wound received from the Vice-President of the United States. His memory will be embalmed with the tears of a nation.

SAME PAPER.

Our country has never felt so severely the dreadful effects of Duelling, as it is likely to experience in that which we are about to announce.

General Hamilton, a man deservedly dear to every worthy citizen of the United States; a man from whom this country has derived benefits more extensive and important than have been conferred upon her by any other man now living; a man, who, viewed in the various relations of scholar, lawyer, soldier, statesman, and citizen, shone with unrivalled splendour; a man whose loss must fill every virtuous mind with the deepest regret; was, on the 11th inst. at Hoboken in Jersey, wounded mortally, in a duel with Col. Burr, Vice-President of the United States.

PORTSMOUTH ORACLE.

Deep lamentation. — Died at New-York, on the afternoon of Thursday last, Gen. *Alexander Hamilton*, of a wound which he received on the morning of the preceding day, in a duel with Col. Burr. Never was a death more sincerely and justly lamented; and his loss will be sensibly felt throughout the United States. In him were united the most splendid talents and the strictest political integrity. There was no man more universally beloved by those who knew him, and in whom such unbounded confidence was placed.

When the feelings of the public shall, in some measure, have subsided, we shall probably present to our readers a correct statement of the circumstances which produced this melancholy event, together with a tribute of respect to the unequalled talents and virtues of that great and illustrious character.

ALBANY CENTINEL.

A numerous and respectable meeting of merchants and other citizens of Albany, convened at the City-Hall of said city, on Friday last at 6 o'clock in the evening, pursuant to public notice, in order " to unite in expressing their sorrow and regret at the loss our country has suffered in the death of its first citizen, Alexander Hamilton."

This meeting being opened, the letter from the Right Rev. Bishop Moore to the Editor of the Evening Post was read, by particular request, and received with a solemn attention, and highly grateful sensations; when the following determinations were adopted:

"WE, the merchants and other citizens of Albany, impressed with a just sense of the merit attached to the character of Alexander Hamilton, by his distinguished military services during the late Revolutionary War — his eminent display of talents and services as a statesman, and his exalted principles of honour and integrity; do feel a deep sense of sorrow and regret at the untimely death of that truly great man; and we do unanimously agree to wear a band of crape around the arm for the space of six weeks, as a testimonial of veneration and esteem for departed merit, and as a badge of mourning for the loss experienced by our country in the death of so invaluable a citizen.

AND we do further agree, that the Clergy of the several denominations in this city, be waited upon, in behalf of this meeting, and requested to preach a Sermon in their respective churches, appropriate to the solemn occasion."

AT a meeting of the Gentlemen of the Bar of this city, it was unanimously agreed to wear crape for six weeks as a testimonial of their veneration and esteem for the talents and virtues of General Hamilton, and of the deep regret with which they deplore his death.

AT a meeting of the Students at Law of the city of Albany, on the 20th of July, 1804, on the occasion of the death of the late Alexander Hamilton — ELIJAH THOMAS in the Chair :

"*Resolved unanimously*, That this meeting entertain the highest veneration for the character, and a lively and sacred respect for the memory of the late Alexander Hamilton ; and that in testimony of their sorrow for his untimely death, they will wear crape on the left arm for six weeks."

TEUNIS VAN VECHTEN, *Sec'ry*.

LANSINGBURGH GAZETTE.

How sleep the Brave! they sink to rest,
By all their country's wishes blest!

Tribute of Respect. — The citizens of Lansingburgh and Waterford, having received the melancholy intelligence of the death of Gen. Alexander Hamilton, met at Johnson's Hotel on Wednesday last, in order to adopt some suitable method of expressing their deep regret for his loss, and the high esteem and veneration which they entertain for his character. . . .

CORNELIUS LANSING, Esq. in the chair ; and John T. Close, secretary.

AFTER some prefatory remarks by David Allen, Esq. in which the virtues of the deceased General were feelingly and impressively portrayed, the following resolutions were unanimously adopted. . . .

"*Resolved*, That this meeting do participate with their fellow-citizens elsewhere, in a due sense of the irreparable loss this state, and the United States, have sustained in the death of Gen. Alexander Hamilton; whose unrivalled talents, distinguished patriotism, eminent services, and unsullied honour, rendered him the ornament of his country.

Resolved also, That as a testimonial of their respect to his memory, they will wear a crape on the left arm for the space of thirty days.

Resolved also, That a committee be appointed to wait on the Rev. Samuel Blatchford, Pastor of the united congregations of Lansingburgh and Waterford, and request him to deliver a Sermon appropriate to the mournful occasion, on Sunday next; and that Elijah Janes, Moses Scott, and David Allen, Esqrs. be that committee."

JOHN T. CLOSE, *Secretary.*

NORTHERN BUDGET.

At a general meeting of the inhabitants of the village of Troy, at Titus' Inn, on the evening of the 17th July, 1804:

" *Resolved unanimously,* That the death of General Alexander Hamilton, whose unrivalled talents and unsullied integrity have exalted him above the reach of Eulogium, is an event to be deplored by all who admire *intelligence,* or venerate *worth.*

2. That, as a testimony of the regret felt by this meeting for the loss of a fellow-citizen so amiable and illustrious, and whose death afflicts *America* and *Humanity,* they will wear crape on the left arm for thirty days.

3. That a committee, composed of N. Schuyler, Wm. M. Bliss, and J. Osborne, Esqrs. wait on the Rev. *Jonas Coe*, and request him to deliver a Discourse, on the next Sabbath, adapted to this solemn occasion."

DERICK LANE, *Chairman.*

Jeremiah Osborne, *Sec'ry.*

Agreeably to the request contained in the above resolution, Mr. Coe delivered, on Sunday afternoon, a Discourse well adapted to the melancholy occasion, from 2. Samuel, 3d chap. and part of the 34th verse — *As a man falleth before wicked men, so fallest thou. And all the people wept for him.* The gloom depicted on the countenances of a very numerous audience, testified the general regret which was excited by the loss of a citizen so eminently useful and honorary to our country.

the bee. (*Democratic.*)

The death of General Hamilton has given his political adversaries, the republicans, an opportunity of displaying a liberality and magnanimity we in vain look for to the federalists. Laying aside the animosity entertained against his political principles, and regarding only his unparalleled talents and accomplishments, the public bodies who have taken up the subject, though composed of republican and federal members, have *unanimously* joined in paying the tribute of respect to his memory. But eminent abilities and integrity are not the peculiar characteristics of contending parties; and when so *great a man* as Alexander Hamilton is suddenly taken off the stage of public action, we should

" Let the good they do live after them."

TESTIMONY OF RESPECT.

At a meeting of the inhabitants of the village of Allentown, in the state of New Jersey, and its vicinity, agreeably to public notice, for the purpose of mutual sympathy and condolence, under the calamity which their country sustains in the distressing and untimely death of her admired and beloved fellow-citizen, General Alexander Hamilton; and for the purpose also of uniting in their *humble* but *sincere* and respectful tribute of admiration and gratitude, so justly due to his memory, his pre-eminent talents, his great and important services as a citizen and soldier, and his many and distinguished virtues — Captain *James Bruere* was chosen Chairman, and *James H. Imlay*, Secretary, when the following resolutions were unanimously adopted:

1st. *Resolved*, That the great and distinguished services and talents, the many and eminent virtues of the late General Alexander Hamilton, have a just claim to the grateful acknowledgement, the high veneration, and the everlasting remembrance and esteem, of his fellow-citizens.

2d. That however questionable may be the correctness of the judgment of the illustrious deceased, in acceding to the interview which led to his afflictive and premature death, we cannot but admire the purity of his motives and the magnanimity of his conduct — and it is with regret at a catastrophe so sad and disastrous, the manner whereof adds accumulated wo to the bitterness of grief, we find ourselves constrained to declare, that there appears no cause for the like admiration of the conduct of his adversary — nor any circumstances connected with that conduct which in any degree alleviate our sorrow, or palliate *so ruthless and vindictive a measure.*

3d. THAT in this afflicting dispensation of Providence, under which our country now mourns, in taking from us our *second Father*, General Alexander Hamilton, the intrepid son and companion of our beloved and venerated *Washington*, in all the toils and dangers of the revolutionary war, and his faithful and confidential friend and counsel in the organization and administration of the general government, we acknowledge the goodness of Heaven in so far prolonging his life as to have afforded him the opportunity to declare his unequivocal disapprobation of the barbarous practice of duelling — and withal to seal and confirm, *with his dying breath, his belief in the essential doctrines of our Holy Religion* — thereby enabling him, to his other excellencies of character, to add the exalted character of a Christian. So that as he was in life, *ambitious only of doing good*, and promoting the *true* and *substantial interests of his country*, in his death it has been his distinguished fortune and felicity alike to subserve this important and desirable object. For himself he had lived enough — to honour and glory. For his country — if her wishes and prayers had prevailed, he had ever lived, while superior talents, inflexible integrity, and distinguished virtue, are estimable in society — nor had he fallen by the *ruthless hand of violence and premeditated revenge.*

4th. THAT the Reverend Mr. Cornell be requested to prepare and deliver a funeral discourse commemorative of his memory and services, exposing the evils of the pernicious custom of duelling, and enforcing also the useful and salutary evidence which the enlightened and comprehensive mind of the deceased hath given of the truth of the Christian Religion.

5th. THAT a copy of the proceedings of this meeting, signed by the Chairman and attested by the Secretary, be published in one or both of the newspapers of Trenton.

JAMES BRUERE, *Chairman.*
JAMES H. IMLAY, *Secretary.*

Allentown, New-Jersey, August 11*th,* 1804.

Trenton, City-Hotel, Sept. 5*th,* 1804.

AT a meeting of the Sergeants, Counsellors, Attornies, and Solicitors of the New-Jersey Bar, at the first term of the Supreme Court since the ever to be lamented fate of General Alexander Hamilton, AARON D. WOODRUFF, Esq. Attorney-General, was called to the chair, and JONATHAN RHEA, Esquire, appointed Secretary:

WHEREUPON it was proposed, and by the Members of the Bar unanimously agreed, in this public manner to join their fellow-citizens throughout the United States, in expressing their deep and most unfeigned grief for the premature death of that unrivalled man.

SENSIBLE that no language of theirs could comprehend his various talents and illustrious actions, and tenderly attached to his well earned fame, they will not diminish its lustre by inadequate conceptions. — In common with the American people, they only unite to publish what they *feel*, that the pride and the hope of their country is for ever lost. This poor and formal tribute to his memory is all that, as a profession, they can bestow — but in each heart there is erected to him a monument, inscribed with perpetual admiration and affection.

PUBLISHED by direction of the New-Jersey Bar,
A. D. WOODRUFF, *Chairman.*
J. RHEA, *Secretary.*

FROM THE CHARLESTON COURIER.

IT may perhaps have occasioned some surprise that we should have hitherto said so little on a subject so deeply affecting to America, and so universally lamented, as the death of Gen. Hamilton. It might have been expected that we, whose political sentiments were so nearly allied to those of that great man, should not be silent on his loss, while every paper on the continent teemed with panegyric, of one kind or other, on the splendour of his talents, and the brilliancy of his virtues. The tribute which enmity itself refuses to the living is very rarely withheld from the dead; for, thank God! the cases are but few in which the human heart is not true to itself: that panegyric should be found most sparing where admiration and respect may have been conceived to be most abundant, will perhaps surprise; but can surprise only those who have not very deeply considered the workings of the soul of man in its strongest emotions.

THAT the illustrious personage at present in contemplation was far beyond the reach of any praise, few will refuse to allow. In that just humility which a sense of the magnitude of the subject, veneration for the man, and the consciousness of our incapacity, inspired, we could not cast a glance at an attempt to delineate such excellence, without drawing back from it with awe —

with fear. Standing in this posture, however, we have had ample occasion to rejoice that the abstinence which arose from instinctive impulse, was as correct as if it had been the result of cool reason and reflection, since the praise of friends so much better qualified for the office than we presume to be, would have thrown our attempts into the shade; and the panegyric of candid men who were his political enemies when he lived, far transcend all that we could hope to offer. The overflowings of our hearts might be taken for the studied panegyric of the partisan; but the praise of generous adversaries carries the stamp of truth upon its face, and has the passport of sincerity to every heart. We could not be wrong in abstaining from an attempt which would put the eloquence of a Flechier, a Mascaron, a Bossuet, or a Burke, to a hard trial, and which is yet performed to greater effect by the sincerity of honest adversaries, than it could by all the eloquence of those great men united, if they were all living, and were, as such men certainly would be, the friends and enthusiastic admirers of General Hamilton.

AMONG those who have done honour to themselves, and indeed to our common nature, by doing justice to General Hamilton, though opposed to his politics, Mr. Cheetham, of New-York, stands eminently foremost. His eulogy upon that illustrious personage is highly creditable to his understanding, and still more creditable to his heart. Rarely have we read a more affecting piece of eloquence. It breathes truth and sincerity in every line. In it the heart is presented to view, as it were, breathless and panting, bursting through the fetters of political prejudice, standing forth to the light of day, and desiring to be understood. Gracious God! how lovely is truth! how eloquent does virtue make men! how dignified the attitude in which Mr. Cheetham stands in that honest effusion — and how much more dignified when contrasted with that *savage part* which he deprecates; which he trusts there is no one man capable of acting; but which we, from the very beginning, expected with something approaching to certainty, would be acted, and which now impudently and ignominiously stares the world in the face.

PERHAPS no illustrious personage, ancient or modern, has ever had a more glorious monument heaped upon his ashes, than General Hamilton has received from the concurrent testimony of all parties, and all characters and descriptions of men in America. His friends and fellow-citizens are inconsolable. The *worthy* men of his adversaries pour forth the voluntary tribute of regret for his death, and panegyric on his life; and the finishing polish, the most brilliant lustre, is given to the whole by the malignity of those biped hyænas, who, as they thirst for the blood of the living, hunger for the flesh of the dead, and purvey for their ravening maws from the recesses of the sepulchre.

THE time has been, when to speak irreverently of the mighty dead, would be looked upon as worse than sacrilege, and when the wretch who carried his animosity beyond the grave, would be hunted down as an alien and enemy to the human race. But the moral world has undergone an earthquake shock, in which the hearts of some have been cast out of their bodies, and cinders raked from the fires of Hell put into their place. What Burke said of the Jacobins and Revolutionists of Europe, may on this occasion be applied to the Jacobins of America. "They have tigers to fall upon animated strength. They have *hyenas* to prey upon dead carcases. The National Menagerie is collected by the first physiologists of the time, and it is defective in no description of *savage* nature. Neither sex nor age — *not the sanctuary of the tomb is sacred to them; and they deny even to the departed, the sad immunities of the grave* — If all Revolutionists [continues he] were not proof against all caution, I should recommend it to their consideration, that no persons were ever known in history, sacred or profane, to *vex the sepulchre*, and by their sorceries to call up the prophetic dead with any other event than the prediction of their own disastrous fate. — *Leave me, oh! leave me to repose.*"

WITH the sentiments of Mr. Cheetham respecting the person who terminated the existence of Gen. Hamilton, we most completely concur. To publish our opinions upon that subject and that person, while he lies under the cloud of unacquitted homicide, would be injustice, and look like a desire to inflame the minds of those who must hereafter try him — *if there be law in this country*. But it may be worth while to ask, *Whether the Chief Magistracy of a country can consistently with law, reason, justice, religion, morality, or common sense, remain deposited in hands embrued in the blood of a fellow-citizen?* Much as we admired General Hamilton, and ardently as we wished to see the magistracy of the potent, yet gentle grasp of his mighty mind, we would have written every pen we have to the stump, to keep him forever from an office of which he would have been morally unfit, if he had in cold-blooded, deliberate malice, taken the life of any citizen, even of Col. Burr. As for this last mentioned gentleman, he may say in the words of Richard, "*Why now my golden dream is out.*" But, so far unlike Richard, he has lost the *bright reward of daring minds* — FOR EVER.

READERS! whatever your political opinions may be, preserve your morals unstained — your hearts unvitiated by malice. What a frightful wreck that man presents to the moral eye, who has silenced the cries of conscience, and stopped the throbs of humanity within his bosom, certain false and malicious observations upon General Hamilton, since his death, disseminated through the papers of America, will show you. Reflect upon them with abhorrence. And as on one hand I conjure you, without reference to political opinions, to applaud Mr. Cheetham for his worthy sentiments, so I beseech you to avert your eyes from the hideous spectacle presented by others, and condemn, but do not curse them.

> Aspicimus populus, quorum non sufficit iræ
> Occidisse aliquem : sed pectora, brachia, vultum
> Crediderint genus esse cibi. JUVENAL, 15th SAT.

> An impious crew we have beheld, whose rage
> Their en'my's very life could not assuage,
> Unless they banquet on the wretch they slew,
> Devour the corpse, and lick the blood they drew !
> DRYDEN'S JUVENAL.

SAME PAPER.

As we are this day called upon, not less by inclination than duty and gratitude, to offer the last public mark of our respect to General Hamilton, it may not be amiss to say a few words respecting that illustrious personage.

IF we make a fair estimate of the value of those great men who have distinguished themselves in this most important era of the history of man, and judge of the services they would hereafter confer, by those they have already rendered to the states; we must consider the death of General Hamilton as the greatest loss, not only which the country has hitherto sustained, but far greater than it is possible for it to sustain at this time, by the death of any single individual. The reverence due to the great champion of our freedom, and founder of our national Independence, Washington, may perhaps give occasion to some people to start with surprise, at a position of such wide and sweeping comprehension, as to the past — while, on the other hand, there will not be wanting those, who, taking their opinions rather from the muddy, green-mantled pool of party prejudice and rancorous faction, than from the pure fountain of wisdom, distributive justice, and truth, will not only question but condemn it. To the former, to whose noble and disinterested sentiments of gratitude for a deceased benefactor, we bow with respect, but not, in this instance, with implicit acquiescence; we say, that the great and glorious being they revere, not more than we do, had accomplished the object of his mission, and fell into the grave by the ordinary visitation of Heaven — ripe in old age and full of honours, venerable with the hoar of many years, and covered with the blessings of a grateful people. He had lived long enough to do all which the wisdom, the valour, and the virtue, of one man could do for his country, and he died time enough to escape that mortifying condition of life, in which the canker of existence and decrepitude eats away the hoarded frame of vigorous manhood, and the trunk, leafless, bare, stripped of its verdant honours, or, perhaps, thunderstruck at the head, bears melancholy testimony of its past grandeur, only by the contrast of its present decay. To wish that

Washington were immortal would be impious, even for Americans — to wish him to live till the rose was withered on the branch, and breathed no smell, would be ungrateful. And here lies the consolation of us all, who, with our posterity, must remain the indefeasible grantees and debtors of the powers of Washington for all we possess; that though his death, let it happen when it would, must have shocked us like some of those natural convulsions which overwhelm our minds with horror while they spare ourselves; yet, now that it has pleased God so to will it that he is gone, we must recollect that he might, in common with some of the greatest men that ever existed, have extended the duration of his life beyond that of his powers, and ere he died, wanted strength to sustain the weight of such a world of dignity and glory as Fortune, for that one occasion, conspiring with supreme virtues and talents, and the best of causes, had laid upon his Atlantean shoulders.

THE state of Hamilton was different; a colossus of might he stood; the American commonwealth on his shoulders; with one foot in the vigour of manhood, and the other in the counsel of ripened years. Whatever services he had done to his country, the growth of his talents, and the mediocrity of his time of life, gave ample hope that he would have done much more. Far from beginning to dwindle, the fruit was not yet at full melioration, and its promised growth and perfection was, to the discerning eye, greater than the past. Superlatively great as he was in retrospect, the eye to which God gives to look into the womb of time, could perceive him greater in prospective: And the Genius of America, if its splendour, glory, and felicity, were her aim, could only have wished that Hamilton were to live, and that an occasion should offer, in which, as has sometimes happened, the nation could be exalted to the highest supremacy of glory by the virtues and talents of one individual.

WHAT did Hamilton want of the essential constituents of a great man? Who is there in the ancient or modern world that, taking in the whole round of human perfections, and moral and patriotic virtues, has surpassed him? And which of the great men who have passed in review before us over the field of history, whose virtues have suffered so little diminution from an alloy, the vices that cling to humanity? We believe none. With the thunder of Demosthenes, the splendour of Cicero, and the patriotic fervour of both, he exhausted his last breath in the service of his country. But, unlike the former, the lustre of his mental endowments was not stained by cowardice or effeminacy. — No Cheronæa witnessed the pusillanimous flight of our American orator. No Træzene or Egina bore testimony to his slothfulness or unmanly indulgence. Nor did he, like the latter, make himself the prominent figure in his own eloquence, or diminish the value of his services by unreasonable or arrogant expectations. As brave, and in sentiment and design as exalted, as the Macedonian Alexander, he was least in his own opinion, exempt from arrogance or pride, and unstained by complexional despotism. With the universal genius of Cæsar, and clemency as signal, but more sincere, no alloy of ambition cheapened the composition of his heart. He abhorred a tyrant as much as Brutus, but he abhorred the use of the poignard more. He was as Cato, just; but unlike Cato, he was severe only to himself. And that mercy which a just sense of the common infirmity of man's nature never fails to infuse into great minds, tempered down to forgiveness his judgments upon every being, and every occasion, but himself and his own conduct.

It is found to be almost beyond the lot of human nature to display any great quality of heart or mind without some counterbalance, some discolouration of infirmity. If we look to the life of this illustrious personage, we shall find more to praise and less to condemn than in almost any other person who has made so distinguished a figure. Men of such stupendous powers, as even his enemies allow he possessed, have seldom been found unadulterated with some foible, some vice, or some oddity, which have detracted from their own general merits, and poisoned, or at least diminished the enjoyments of those about them. Johnson was rude, overbearing, and insufferable to all (and they were but few) who levelled with him, unless they had the misfortune to deserve from his pity what they could not obtain from his politeness. Newton was absent, and enveloped from society in clouds of abstraction. Swift was furious, sneering, harsh, and fastidious. The elder Pitt was, from excessive, capricious passion, at times the curse of his house. In short, if we examine the lives of almost all great men, we shall find them frail, feeble, and extravagant; odd and capricious in some points, in proportion to the magnitude of their powers and perfections; and the splendour of their talents in others. Not so our illustrious warrior and statesman, Hamilton. High in science, he displayed it not unnecessarily; and when he did, disclosed it with such humility and diffidence, as if he felt his superiority to be only an adventitious circumstance, for which it was his duty rather to be humbly thankful to God who gave it, than proudly overbearing to his creatures — and as if he considered the talents he possessed the property of his fellow-citizens, confided by the Giver of all to his care, to be dealt out to them not as his own and as a favour, but as their property, deposited in his keeping for their use. In the pursuits of an arduous and abstruse professional science, he never suffered himself to be caught napping in the contemptuous affectation of absence, or bewildered in real or pretended abstraction; never was found peevish from interruption, hasty from opposition, or supercilious from consciousness of superiority. The friend, the fellow-citizen, the stranger who approached him, found the same serene equanimity and suavity at all times portrayed in his manners, beaming from his countenance, and dropping from his lips. — Those lips on which the Bees of Hybla perched while he was yet cradled. — Wife, children, friends, domestics, dependants, were made by the sweetness, the tender humility, the wise playfulness, and the eternally unruffled cheerfulness of the man, to forget what every one else knew, namely, that they were then in contact with one of the greatest of mankind. He lived, and as he lived he died, a creature of the public, devoted to its service.

No man was more teemingly filled with that enthusiasm which distinguished the Roman breast, and animated the heroes of that republic to the performance and achievements which we contemplate at this day with astonishment, doubt, and admiration; with that patriotic enthusiasm which glowed in the bosom of Curtius, of Regulus, and of the Decii, and impelled them to devote their lives a willing sacrifice to the good of their country.

INDEED, it is hard to tell which was most conspicuous in this extraordinary man — the splendour and usefulness of his public talents, or the happy effects of his private virtues. Energetic, disinterested, perspicacious, penetrating, strenuous, and intrepid, he discharged his public functions with unrivalled greatness, and without ostentation : mild, gentle, affable, sincere, unassuming, full of simple grace and natural dignity, he was unsurpassed in the discharge of the social duties, in every relation of domestic life, insomuch that those who only heard his eloquence at the bar, or at the public tribunals, or saw his deeds of enterprise as a soldier, would conclude he was born for that particular situation alone; while those who witnessed his life at *the hearth*, wou'1 swear that to plunge him in the storms of public conṯntion, was to misapply the man, and to rob private socie. of one of its highest ornaments and greatest blessings.

We will not break in upon the sanctity of this hallowed day,* with any observations unworthy of the occasion, or contradictory to the spirit of mildness, meekness, charity, and christian benevolence, which was the soul of the inimitable Hamilton. We will only say — Americans! you have lost your champion, your counsellor, and your guide. The ornament of your country is destroyed — the lustre of your state is extinguished. The head that guided your guides — that clearest head that ever conceived, and that sweetest tongue that ever uttered the dictates of wisdom, which confounded your foes and enlightened your councils, is now mouldering to clay. That arm which from youth to death was ready raised to fall upon and crush the heads of your enemies, is now melting to a clod of the valley. And that heart which braved and fluttered even Britons, when Britons were your foes;

* The day devoted to a public testimonial of respect for Hamilton's memory, by the citizens of Charleston.

which now poured forth its might in a torrent of terror upon armed hosts, and again flowed in heavenly mercy to the conquered and prostrate, is by the hand of hatred and ruthless vengeance, given to the worms. Yes, Hamilton is gone, for ever gone! No more shall his valour and military virtues flash confusion in the face of your enemies; no more his sagacious and perspective wisdom guide your councils; to you all those blessings are lost; from you they are outrageously torn. Yet, fellow-citizens, profit by his death, as you have profited by his life. Let it awaken you from that drunken dream in which you have wasted away your honour, your morals, and your religion — and, alas! given to the grave — sent to eternity for a mere temporary offence, so many of your fellow-creatures. Fellow-citizens, let it produce in your hearts a wholesome horror of deeds of blood; and let it open every channel of your souls, while in sincerity we pour into them this undeniable truth, that killing by duel is inexpiable murder, against condemnation for which no worldly custom, no fashionable habit, will be allowed by God as a plea in bar. That to take the life of another on any account but real self-defence, is a crime to which God, being all just, cannot extend mercy: that you deceive yourselves when you imagine a weapon levelled at you by mutual agreement with an antagonist, affords the plea of self-defence: for that on the contrary, it enhances the damnable crime of murder by the still more damnable, if more damnable were possible, crime of suicide. It is no time to palter with this great moral question now, when such examples are before us. The legislators who do not oppose terrible penal laws to the perpetration of murder by duel, are accessories before the fact to those who commit that crime. And those who would not execute the laws, if made, and terrify the community from such a crime by repeated victims, would be in fact murderers themselves.

Devote this day to pious contemplation, suitable to the melancholy event — let your contemplation bring forth fruits of amendment, and let Hamilton be your example in every thing but in the *mode* of his death.

SAME PAPER.

The universal shock which the death of Gen. Hamilton has given to this country from one end to the other, sufficiently denotes the sense entertained of his extraordinary merits and greatness ; of the services he had done, and the services expected from him. The full extent and magnitude of the loss sustained by his death, few optics are able to measure ; and none can imagine, but those who are capable of knowing how much the wisdom of one man may do for a nation, or even for the good of the whole world ; and who at the same time know the almost unfathomable depth of that great man's mind. It seems, however, as if it was ordained by Heaven, that nothing belonging to him should be useless to his country and his fellow-creatures, since even that most dreadful calamity, his death, is likely in one respect to be beneficial to them. It has roused and set in motion the almost extinguished sense of humanity, which once rendered the murder of a fellow-creature a subject of unutterably horrible contemplation.

Duelling is now looked upon with something like the detestation it deserves ; and will in all probability be put not only under the anathema of the general heart and mind of the country, but under the heavy penalty of the law. If those vices are most dangerous to society which assume the exterior appearance of excellence, and simulate virtue, duelling ought to be treated with greater rigour than common murder, since it carries with it circumstances, which, to young, to light, and to superficial minds, and above all, to the boastful and vain glorious fool, render it so seductive as to overcome all scruples of conscience, all feeling for a fellow-creature, all sense of duty to God, and, what with some wretches is more extraordinary, all sense of their own danger. For these reasons, and since the voice of all mankind is already raised with just and unmitigated abhorrence and vengeance, against the perpetrator of every other mode or species of murder, the law should assume an aspect of tenfold terror to the duellist, and put him by a deep, strongly written, black, unalterable letter, out of the pale of human mercy, and offer him up an expiatory sacrifice for the many thousands of murders which cry to heaven for vengeance on the country that suffered such deeds to be done, and let its laws lie passive.

> "When by just vengeance guilty mortals perish,
> "The gods behold their punishment with pleasure,
> "And lay the uplifted thunderbolt aside."
>
> ADDISON.

EXCLUSIVE of the sin of murder, duelling has other ruinous circumstances attending it — ruinous to the prosperity and peace of whole families; ruinous to the morals, well being, and peace of society; and ruinous to the common weal, as being often the instrumental agent of faction, and corrupting the very first principle of our constitutional freedom, and destroying the freedom of election.

[THE foregoing elegant productions, from the Charleston Courier, containing many striking, correct, and original observations, are from the warm heart and clear head of Mr. S. CULLEN CARPENTER, editor of that paper; a gentleman whose pen has justly gained him celebrity throughout the United States. It was his happiness personally to know him whose virtues and transcendent talents he has here so eloquently described.]

THE following elegant and pathetic effusion is from the pen of Mr. Lathrop, editor of the Utica Patriot:

DEATH OF GENERAL HAMILTON.

> "When the bright guardians of a country die,
> The grateful tear in tenderness will start;
> And the keen anguish of a reddening eye,
> Disclose the deep afflictions of the heart!"

To swell the sable triumphs of the tomb, the great Destroyer, in pointing his shaft at Hamilton, has selected a victim of no ordinary value. He has not only taken from the bosom of a beloved family its solace and support; from the circle of his immediate friends its pride and ornament; from the forum its most distinguished advocate; from society an eminent and useful citizen; but from his country he has taken its ablest statesman, its warmest patriot, its great benefactor.

WITH talents of a superior order, the choicest in nature's gift, improved by an elegant and refined education, strengthened by intense and laborious application, directed to usefulness by a steady love of justice and an undeviating adherence to the cause of truth, as a soldier, a statesman, a public advocate, a warm friend and zealous guardian of the liberties of his country; the invaluable life of this distinguished citizen has been spent with increasing glory to himself, and incalculable usefulness to his country.

As a member of the family of the illustrious Washington; as his companion in arms; as his counsellor and friend, he shared with him the dangers of the revolution, and reaped with him the glory of its accomplishment. The siege of York-Town, which closed the military operations of the country, witnessed the last brilliant display of his military skill and unyielding bravery. As a soldier, he united bravery with humanity, skill with activity. So eminently distinguished were his military talents, that he was designated on a momentous occasion by the great Washington himself, as the man of his choice, to take the active command of our armies.

As a statesman, the astonishing powers of his mind had full scope for exertion, and he has left the most splendid testimony of their extent and usefulness. With talents profound and active, with genius acute and penetrating, with learning deep and extensive, he made unwearied researches in political science, and has left as a rich legacy to his countrymen, a luminous view of the most correct principles in civil policy and government. As a minister of finance and a constitutional counsellor of the executive, he shone with peculiar greatness. The fiscal regulations of our country witness his versatile and extraordinary powers, in the speedy acquisition and practical improvement of the principles of science, new and intricate. Called by a beloved President to raise the sinking credit of a nation, to explore its resources, and direct its finances to an effective application, we were astonished at the facility with which he accomplished this arduous undertaking.

As an advocate at the bar, he was unrivalled. He had drained the deepest fountains of legal science, and from the more pleasing source of belles-letters learning he had acquired the most commanding eloquence. In the practice of professional duty, he became the good man's friend and advocate, a terror to the oppressor, and a foe to iniquity.

> "He was never found to pluck down justice
> From its awful bench,
> To trip the cause of law, or blunt the sword
> That guards the peace and safety of the state."

In the private walks of life, through all its relative duties, Hamilton was highly valued....

> "His life was gentle, and the elements so mixt
> In him, that nature might stand up and say
> To all the world — *this was a man*."

But to be the pride of his country and its chief ornament, availed him nothing! Neither his greatness, nor his usefulness, could avert the impending blow, or wrest from its purposes the counsels of the Almighty.

> "Ah! what avail'd that wide capacious mind,
> With every science accurately fraught,
> The keen ey'd fancy spark'ling and refin'd,
> The blaze of genius and the burst of thought?
> Ah! what avail'd that magnitude of soul,
> Warm'd to debate by patriotic fire,
> Which bade the bolts of eloquence to roll,
> And taught astonish'd senates to admire?
> Bade his lov'd country shake away the gloom,
> Which bound her feeble temples with disgrace;

> And like the bold, but deathless chief of Rome,
> Twine everlasting laurels in its place?
> Ah! nought avail'd the mind's extended power,
> Nor worth, nor greatness, could avert his doom;
> Snatch'd in the sun-beam swiftness of an hour,
> To swell the triumphs of th' insatiate tomb."

YES, reader, this brilliant luminary in the literary world, this splendid orb of our political hemisphere, is set for ever! A star of the first magnitude in the political temple is extinguished! A Pillar of superior strength is fallen! Cut off in the full vigour of life, in the full possession of his faculties, and in the midst of all his usefulness, the great Hamilton now sleeps with his fathers! That intellectual fountain, from which flowed the richest streams of eloquence, is dried up; the fire of that genius, whose acuteness pierced the inmost recesses of science, is quenched for ever; that eye, whose penetrating glance was the sure index of an acute and penetrating mind, is now closed for ever; that tongue, on whose eloquence listening senates hung with admiration, is now silent for ever; and dumb for ever is that voice which was the harbinger of wisdom, and the herald of instruction. The trophies of the grave are enriched with a gem of superior worth; the world is rifled of an intellectual treasure of inestimable value.

> "O! what a fall was there, my countrymen!
> Then you and I, and all of us fell down,
> Whilst *bloody treason* triumph'd over us."

THOUGH the grave now shrouds the mortal part of the now immortal Hamilton, his memory and his fame are enshrined in the bosoms of his grateful countrymen, and will be ever cherished and protected, with the warmest emotions of love and admiration. This sacred deposit will be transmitted to posterity in the fulness of its glory and the purity of its excellence. A distinguished page in the annals of our country, will be adorned with the record of his character, with a faithful delineation of his talents, virtues, achievements, and greatness, and the admiration of posterity shall perpetuate his fame. There will the record of the sad catastrophe of his death draw forth the tear of pity from the eye of tenderness, and the sigh of regret from the bosom of humanity. There will the moralist read with warm approbation the sentiments of a Hamilton, on the subject of the barbarous custom to which he fell a sacrifice; there will he see the abhorrence in which he held a practice, sanctioned by the manners of the age in which he lived; and which, from a peculiar combination of circumstances, he conceived as to himself was unavoidable. There will the Christian dwell with exquisite delight on the record of the bright example of this great man, who, in the fulness of belief, embraced the doctrines of christianity, partook of its ordinances, and died in the consoling hope of its promises.

FROM THE BOSTON REPERTORY.

TEARS OF COLUMBIA.

ALTERED FROM COLLINS.

WHILE lost to all her former mirth,
Columbia, weeping, bends to earth,
   And seeks her *Hero's* grave —
While stain'd with blood, she strives to tear,
Unseemly, from her fragrant hair
   The wreaths that *Summer* gave:

The thoughts that musing *Pity* pays,
And fond *Remembrance* loves to raise,
  Shall on her steps attend;
Still *Fancy*, to herself unkind,
Awakes to grief the soften'd mind,
  And paints the bleeding friend.

By *Hudson's* broad descending wave
Her ceaseless tears bedew the grave,
  Where *Hamilton* is laid —
That *sacred spot*, with cypress crown'd,
Shall jealous *Honour* watch around,
  And *Truth* protect the shade.

O'er him whose doom thy virtues grieve,
Aerial forms shall sit at eve,
  And bend the pensive head;
And fall'n by fate's severe command,
Imperial *Honour's* awful hand
  Shall point his lowly bed.

The warlike dead of ev'ry age,
Who fill the fair recording page,
  Shall leave their sainted rest —
And half reclining on his spear,
Each wond'ring chief by turns appear
  To hail the blooming guest.

Great *Washington*, unknown to yield;
Montgomery, from *Abram's field* —
  Shall gaze with fix'd delight;
Again their Country's wrongs they feel;
Again they snatch the gleaming steel,
  And wish th' avenging fight.

But lo! where sunk in deep despair,
Her garment torn, her bosom bare,
  Impatient *Freedom* lies!

Her matted tresses madly spread,
To ev'ry sod which wraps the dead,
  She turns her joyless eyes.

If weak to sooth thy soften'd heart,
These pictur'd glories nought impart
  To dry thy constant tear;
If yet in sorrow's distant eye,
Expos'd and pale thou see'st him lie,
  Where *Greenwich shades* appear!—

Where'er from time thou court'st relief,
The Muse shall still with social grief,
  With thee her vigils keep:
Ev'n *Vernon*'s lone sepulchral vale
Shall learn the sad respected tale,
  Where sainted relicks sleep.

FROM THE ALEXANDRIA DAILY ADVERTISER.

AN ACROSTIC.

H ark! how the toilsome noise of busy trade,
A mid wan sorrow's heart-felt sighs, is lost;
M ark how the hero and the tender maid
I n tears unite to mourn their country's boast;
L ong has the fiend-like custom bath'd in wo
T he Heav'n taught soul, the pure celestial eye—
O let it now to felon despots go,
N or may in vain the peerless patriot die!

FROM THE ALBANY CENTINEL.

THE fall of Gen. Hamilton, with its attending circumstances, is one of the most interesting events which the human mind can contemplate. He was perhaps the most finished character in the world; certainly there is not one of his contemporaries, however great and celebrated, who unites so many and various qualifications. Of his military talents there needs no other proof, than the confidence placed in him by Washington, and the services in which he employed him during the revolutionary war. His wonderful intellectual resources, the extent and acuteness of his observation, the nobleness of his spirit, qualified him to command and to conquer. Had he been called to act on a military theatre commensurate with the greatness of his genius, the splendours of his military character would have equalled those of the most celebrated heroes. As a *Statesman* and *Politician*, he stands among the first and greatest the world has yet seen. He was the vital principle of the first administration under the constitution; and for the establishment of that constitution we were more indebted to him than to any other man. Without his *Herculean* efforts, it is probable that it would not have been adopted; that we never would have experienced the benefits of that union to which we owe our national greatness. It is not improper nor extravagant praise to say, that his *Federalist* and his debates in our State Convention, indicate an acquaintance with the science of politics superior to any thing that can be found in any political work extant. The subject of the *Federalist* was *peculiarly* interesting *here*; hence, perhaps, it is not so generally known in Europe as it deserves to be. If this great work was better known abroad, Hamilton would doubtless be thought unrivalled as a political writer. In estimating his political character, his *Phocion* and *Camillus* should not be forgotten.

As a *Civilian* and a *Lawyer*, his country has not his equal — nor is it probable, that *Westminster-Hall* can boast of his superior. The wonderful analytical powers of his mind, fitted him for singular excellence in his profession. Whatever may be allowed to the *eloquence* of Mr.

Erskine, there is not at the English Bar, as far as we are able to describe, *so great a man* as Hamilton.

As an *Orator*, those who knew him, and who are acquainted with the performances of the most celebrated public speakers of ancient and modern times, will rank him among the most able of those who have ever exercised the arts of convincing and persuading. The most admired performances of Pitt and Fox, the first public speakers in Great-Britain, do not indicate greater extent, more richness of mind, or elegance of manner, than the every-day speeches of Hamilton. No man possessed a more admirable power to engage and preserve the attention of his audience. Such was the singular propriety of his elocution, such the fascination of his manner, that after pouring forth the abundance of his thoughts for many successive hours, every ear yet heard him — every eye was yet fixed upon him. He generally addressed himself only to the understanding: yet he could animate, and warm, and melt. In the pathetic, he was indeed always successful. Sometimes he would play a little, and the elegance of his pleasantry, was not the least part of his excellence. Those whose opportunities to hear him were frequent, have lost a pleasure beyond all price. There was something in the air and port of Hamilton, uncommonly majestic and sublime. His manners and address were courteous and humane. He was well fitted to be a popular leader, and would have dignified and graced a throne. He was eloquent as Pericles, amiable and brave as Francis I. or Henry IV. and more enlightened than either.

PERHAPS no man's death has ever occasioned so much affliction. When Washington died, Hamilton was left.

Our country grieves for the loss of her pride, her ornament, her boast, her hope, her DEFENCE. But independent of the public calamity, each individual is personally afflicted, and feels that he is deprived of something near and dear to him.

WITH respect to the motives, views, and expectations of Mr. Burr, those who are acquainted with the characters and tempers of the parties, and who have attentively considered the correspondence that preceded the fatal interview, can have but one opinion. This duel has occasioned a sore public calamity, and much private affliction. To Mr. Burr it has brought misery and ruin. His character now is no *better*, than it was before the death of General Hamilton, whose blood has not washed away its stains! And all office, public honours, power, and trust, are now for ever out of the reach of Aaron Burr!

SAME PAPER.

SUNDAY last was devoted, by the citizens of the village of Salem, (N. Y.) to the grateful and soul-approving purpose of contributing their manifestation of regret, at the untimely death, and irreparable loss of our friend and first citizen, Gen. *Alexander Hamilton;* whose courage aided to found, and whose wisdom protected this widespreading and growing republic. For this purpose, a very numerous and respectable portion of the inhabitants of the village attended at the Meeting-House, where the Rev. Alexander Proudfit delivered a Sermon, pertinent to the afflicting occasion, from this passage of Scripture: "*Now* SAMUEL *was dead and all Israel had lamented him,* "*and buried him in* Ramah, *even in his own city.*" In which the inflexible patriotism, and the exemplary social virtues of the illustrious deceased, were exhibited in a truly im-

pressive manner — as was evinced by the deep gloom
which overspread the countenances of the audience.

"Each age to HIM its grateful dues shall pay,
"And join with us to mourn his fun'ral day."

THOUGH so much has already appeared in the papers relative to the death of Gen. Hamilton, we cannot deny ourselves the pleasure of republishing the following handsome paragraph from the Palladium, a democratic paper, printed in Frankfort, Kentucky. It is introductory to a compendious statement of the causes which led to the dreadful catastrophe. — *Gaz. U. S.*

"THE death of Gen. Hamilton, who lately fell in a duel with Col. Burr, has excited more public sensibility, than any circumstance which has occurred since the death of Washington. The finer feelings of the soul, which it has awakened, appear to have extinguished the resentment of party; and if this has been the effect upon his political opponents, how inadequate must be the power of language to describe the sensations so afflicting an event must produce in the bosoms of his friends? His transcendent talents, actively exerted for a number of years in favour of federal politics, pointed him out as the most distinguished leader of the party — by whom his loss is, no doubt, very sincerely deplored. Indeed, it is irreparable."

FROM THE BOSTON CENTINEL.

WASHINGTON'S CHARACTER OF HAMILTON.

Middlesex, August 13, 1804.

MR. RUSSELL,

THE newspapers have lately been filled with accounts of the sad event at New-York, and with characteristic traits of the illustrious victim therein: These publications are calculated to do much good in society. They have developed the character, services, and patriotism, of a citizen, whose fame has been assailed by every "puny whipster" that could guide a pen. Nor has even the grave, which, in the magnanimous, always bars the gates of enmity, shielded the Patriot from the upbraidings of ignorance and vileness. The deceased is still reproached with incivism, with ambition. Let us examine those reproaches:— His incivism has been displayed in his being one of the framers of the present constitution of the United States; and, though a bold word, the MOST ABLE and indefatigable advocate for its adoption and execution. To the charge of ambition, let WASHINGTON speak: That Washington, whom the democrats pretended to venerate; and whom they dare not cease to eulogize in their toasts, and their rhapsodies: That Washington whose discriminating talents were ever acknowledged; who was honest as independent, and independent as inflexible.

LET every citizen who desires to see the truth; let every one who can read, read the following extract of a letter from General Washington to Mr. Adams, when President of the United States. CIVIS.

GENERAL WASHINGTON TO PRESIDENT ADAMS.

"*Mount-Vernon, Sept.* 25, 1798.

"IT is an invidious task, at all times, to draw comparisons, and I shall avoid it as much as possible; but I have no hesitation in declaring, that if the public is to be deprived of the services of Col. Hamilton in the military line, the post he was destined to fill will not easily be supplied — and that this is the sentiment of the public, I think I may venture to pronounce. Although Col. Hamilton has never acted in the character of a general officer, yet his opportunities, as the *principal and most confidential aid* of the Commander in Chief, afforded him the means of viewing every thing on a larger scale than those who had only divisions and brigades to attend to ; who knew nothing of the correspondences of the Commander in Chief, or of the various orders to, or transactions with, the general staff of the army. These advantages, and his having served with usefulness in the old Congress, in the General Convention, and having filled one of the most important departments of government with acknowledged abilities and integrity, have placed him on high ground ; and made him a conspicuous character in the United States, and even in Europe. To these, as a matter of no small consideration, may be added, that as a lucrative practice in the line of his profession is his most certain dependence, the inducement to relinquish it must in some degree be commensurate. By some he is considered as an *ambitious* man, and therefore a dangerous one. That he is *ambitious* I shall readily grant, but it is of that *laudable kind, which prompts a man to excel in whatever he takes in hand.*

" He is enterprising — quick in his perceptions — and his judgment intuitively great: qualities essential to a great military character; and therefore I repeat, *that his loss will be irreparable.*

" GEORGE WASHINGTON."

The affectionate and elegant tribute from ' Jaques,' to the memory of Hamilton, is entitled to a much higher place in literary estimation, than those vulgar wailings which usually deform our Gazettes, and '*petrify* one, in a single stanza.'—*Dennie.*

FROM THE PORT FOLIO.

REFLECTIONS IN SOLITUDE.

JAQUES ON HAMILTON.

In solitude, though Rumour's aspen tongue,
May ring upon the ear her changing notes,
Yet oft, like fleeting forms which Fancy calls
To build the morning dreams which lovers know,
They pass away, and busy Mem'ry bears
But faint impression of the idle sounds!
Yet oft, when Silence sleeps upon the leaves,
Intrusive Rumour wakes me from my dreams
With tales so mournful, and so oft repeated,
That e'en in solitude I may not choose
But sorrow, and the heart, responsive still,
Murmurs the melancholy tale to air!
Oh! then, to startled Fancy's sickened vision,
The morning music of the robin dies,
The brook's pure waters stagnate in their course,
And the green foliage of the lofty woods
Assumes a sickly cast. Suspicion then
Steals to my ear, and whispers me to shun
The harmless peasant lurking near my haunts,
Intent on blood. Contagion too takes wing
From crowded streets, and flying on the breeze,
Rears many a sod, and rudely sculptured stone
Within the grave-yard of the village church!
Rumour! with all thy hundred busy tongues,
Thou can'st not tell a tale so sorrowful
To pierce my country's heart, as that which late
The sighs of millions breath'd upon my ear!
Oft may a parent, while his orphans mourn,
Sleep with his fathers in the mouldering tomb;
Yet kind Oblivion soon will chase the tear
From swelling lids; for Pleasure's gaudy beam

Dries Sorrow's source, as I have often seen
The vernal brook escape from summer suns.
Humanity has ceaseless cause to weep,
For '*man was made to mourn.*' So sang the bard,
Whom, when the Muses left their sacred groves,
To claim the mortal who had stol'n their lyre,
They found on Scotia's music-gifted hills
Warbling a song of sweetest minstrelsy —
While round his plough the wondering peasants flock'd.
Athens her orator — her *Cæsar*, Rome
Have mourned: Her noble *Chatham*, Albion mourns,
And Sparta's honours gather round the grave
Beneath whose turf Leonidas was laid.
These men were great, and good, and merited
The fairest honours, and the warmest tears.
Thou too, my country! hast a debt to pay,
Of which Peruvian mines were poor to rid thee!
No! let thy lips dwell ceaseless on the name;
Let thy warm tears bedew the yet green grave,
And let the laurels, which thy love may plant,
Thicken around the fame of HAMILTON.
For he was thine, and only thine, my country!
Thy fields attest his valour in thy cause;
Thy senate hung in rapture on his lips,
Which poured as sweet a stream of eloquence
As Athens knew. Full many a sleepless night
His thorny pillow own'd the sighs and tears
Which heaved and streamed for thee, and thee alone!
And in that deed, which laid his bosom bare,
As Honour whisper'd him, he lent his ear,
And, fancying, heard his country claim his life!
Spirit of Genius! Oh! had I that glow
Of intellect, which late illum'd thy soul,
And prov'd Promethean fire no fabled song:
I then should muse, for friendship's partial ears,
Strains not unworthy of thy bright'ning fame!
Yet to thy country still that fame is dear,
And HE, who form'd thee good as thou wert great,
May prompt some pen to sketch each glorious deed
That mark'd thy days. Then shall th' historic page

Record thee as thou wert. Thy val'rous acts
Shall lead the youthful warrior to the field,
Who still shall copy thee, and stay his sword
When Mercy sues. In academic shades,
When youth shall dwell upon that eloquence,
Which Greece alone had rivalled, he shall feel
Ambition lightning all her glowing fires —
His heart shall throb — his feeble pulses swell —
His bright eye kindle, and, with rapid glance,
Dart on the page devoted to thy fame;
And as he gazes on the envied height,
Which thou hadst early reach'd, he yet may deem
It well befitting his advent'rous flight
To seat him there. Some youthful Solon too,
Whom fate may lead to build an empire up,
Shall gather wisdom from thy lum'nous mind,
Which saw its country, even at its birth,
Fast sinking to the tomb where states repose,
And, nobly rescuing it from Faction's grasp,
Pointed the path to Honour and to Fame.
The page of Hist'ry, too, with pride shall tell,
That when the treasures of thy country lay
Within thy easy grasp, they could not tempt
Thy honest soul. Oh! it shall proudly say,
' Lo! his grey hairs announc'd the hour of rest,
Yet Poverty still claim'd him as her child!'
The simple narrative, which Truth shall tell,
Shall prove thy brightest, fairest eulogy!
Time, as he steals along, and ceaseless yields
Fictitious greatness to Oblivion's tomb,
Shall own thy fame superior to his power,
And feel the splendour that encircles thee!
The foes of Virtue, HAMILTON! were thine,
And thine her dearest friends! She lesson'd thee,
When Pleasure's syrens wanton'd in thy path,
To fix thy steady eye on Honour's form,
And deem the hours misspent, which found thee not
Thy country's *Mentor;* and she promis'd thee
The sweetest recompense for all thy toils,
Which Virtue gives, and souls like thine desire;

For know, when truth shall dissipate the gloom,
Which faction thickened to obscure thy fame,
That thou shalt find, wherever Honour lives,
Hearts warm, lips busy, and remembrance prompt,
To speak of one, whose bosom knew no guile.
                                          JAQUES.

END OF NO. IV.

A COLLECTION, &c.

―※―

Nº. V.

INTERESTING LETTER.

The following highly interesting letter from General Pinckney, it must be recollected, comes from a gentleman of the most liberal mind, a soldier of the nicest honour, and of tried and unquestionable bravery. This consideration will, we are sure, give to his sentiments on the subject of duelling, the greatest possible weight throughout the community. Should the death of Hamilton be the cause of bringing into merited disgrace the disorganizing sentiment, that "a gentleman's honour is under the protection of his *own arm*," and that instead of appealing to the laws, he is to look for vengeance to private force; and if it shall be the means of scouting from our country the absurd, unjust, and murderous practice of taking life itself for even imaginary offences to imaginary honour — " then indeed will not a Hamilton have died in vain."

At a Meeting of the Standing Committee of the Society of the Cincinnati of the State of New-York, on Wednesday, 5th of Sept. 1804:

The President presented a letter received by him from Major General *Charles Cotesworth Pinckney*, Vice-President-General of the Society of the Cincinnati, which was read and attentively considered — Whereupon, resolved unanimously, That this Committee highly approve the sentiments expressed in the said letter, and that the Secretary forthwith cause the same to be published.

The President also presented a letter from Mrs. *Hamilton*, which was also read — Resolved unanimously, that the Secretary cause the same to be published.

WM. POPHAM, Sec'ry.

Charleston, S. C. August 18, 1804.

Sir,

With deep affliction, I received the account of our irreparable loss by the death of our late President-General. This deplorable event has been sensibly felt and lamented in this part of the union, even by those who were not personally acquainted with him, and who did not coincide with him in politics. By me, who have witnessed his calm intrepidity and heroic valour, on trying occasions, and was acquainted with his transcendent abilities and amiable qualities, and honoured with his particular friendship, his loss is most poignantly felt, and his memory will be ever most affectionately revered.

Is there no way of abolishing, throughout the Union, this absurd and barbarous custom, to the observance of which he fell a victim? Duelling is no criterion of bravery; for I have seen cowards fight duels, and I am convinced real courage may often be better shown in the refusal than in the acceptance of a challenge. If the Society of Cincinnati were to declare their abhorrence of this practice, and the determination of all their members to discourage it as far as they had influence, and on no account either to send or accept a challenge, it might tend to annul this odious custom, and would be a tribute of respect to the sentiments and memory of our late illustrious Chief. If the State Society of New-York should coincide with me in opinion, I should be glad to have their sentiments, how best to carry it into execution; whether by submitting it to a meeting of the General Society at New-York, Philadelphia, or Baltimore, or by referring the matter at once to the different State Societies, for their consideration.

I HAVE this day received your favour of the 25th of July, and am much obliged to the State Society, and to yourself, for it. With sentiments of great respect, I have the honour to be,
    Your most obedient servant,

    CHARLES COTESWORTH PINCKNEY,
                                    V. P. G. S. C.

Col. W. S. SMITH, President of the New-York
    State Society of the Cincinnati.

THE following letter from Mrs. Hamilton will excite the sympathies of those who feel for her individual loss, and in it lament a great national calamity.

                        Albany, August 11, 1804.
SIR,
    To the distress of a heart so deeply afflicted as mine, from the irreparable loss of a most amiable and affectionate husband, I trust the respectable society in which you preside, will impute the delay of an acknowledgment

for their consolatory letter, couched in terms that evince their sympathy emanates from the heart.

Although great mitigation of that affliction, with which I am so severely depressed, can only be hoped from the mercies of the Divine Being, in whose dispensations it is the duty of his creatures humbly and devoutly to acquiesce; yet, the wounded heart derives a degree of consolation from the tenderness with which its lot is bewailed, by the virtuous, the wise, and humane — and also from that high honour and respect with which the memory of the dear deceased has been commemorated by them, and those contemplated in the resolutions of the Society of the Cincinnati, transmitted by you, and for which you, Sir, will be pleased to convey my warmest thanks to that respectable body.

I reciprocate with sensibility your and their recommendation of me to the Divine care and protection — May they ever enjoy it, and without alloy.

I am, Sir, with great respect,
Your obedient servant,
E. HAMILTON.

To William S. Smith, Esq.

FROM THE ALBANY CENTINEL.

A BRIEF REVIEW

OF THE PUBLIC LIFE AND WRITINGS OF

GENERAL HAMILTON.

While the public are every where lamenting the untimely fate of this great and excellent character, and bestowing on his memory the deepest expressions of veneration and gratitude, I have found a melancholy but tender consolation in endeavouring to recal to memory the principal actions of his illustrious life. His efforts in the public service were disinterested, unremitting, and manly; and his views the most penetrating and comprehensive. It is from a review of his political life and writings that we perceive and feel the more strongly, the wonderful extent, strength, and activity of his mind, and the ardour and purity of a heart devoted to the public welfare.

GENERAL HAMILTON entered the army in the beginning of the American war, and while he was still a youth. He was soon taken into General Washington's family as one of his aids, and with the rank of Lieutenant-Colonel. He was with the Commander in Chief in that character at the battle of Monmouth, in June, 1778. General Washington, in one of his official letters to Congress at that time, says, that Lieutenant Col. Hamilton was "well informed of his sentiments on every point;" and he has since declared in writing, that "Col. Hamilton was his principal and most confidential aid." He commanded the American detachment that carried by assault one of the enemy's redoubts at the siege of York-Town, in the evening of the 14th October, 1781. This was a small but brilliant affair, and noted at the time for the rapidity with which it was conducted, and the humanity that crowned the victors.

THE capture of Cornwallis was the last great act of the revolutionary war, and Col. Hamilton immediately turned his attention to the profession of the law. But the duties of that profession were always with him a secondary object, and he immediately entered upon that course of action in the civil department of government, in which he was destined by providence to act a part so eminently useful and glorious. In July, 1782, he was chosen a member of Congress by the Legislature of this state, and in the ensuing session of the winter of 1783, the proceedings of Congress were stamped with a new and striking character. This is visible to every observer, who will take the pains of perusing and comparing their journals. Their reports and resolutions were luminous and masterly, both for matter and style. Congress made new, vigorous, and persevering efforts, to give the confederation all the force of which that languid constitution was susceptible, by endeavouring to command resources competent to rear up and establish the prostrate credit of the union. It would not, however, be just or decorous to impute this renewed energy, this unusual discernment and anxiety which were conspicuous in the national councils, exclusively to the presence of any particular member. But this much is certain, that Mr. Hamilton took an early and distinguished *lead* in all the prominent measures of the session. He moved the resolution, pressing the states to comply with the money requisitions, "*in order to render justice to the public creditors;*" and in this he early announced that great ruling principle of probity and policy, which he pursued through the whole course of his political life. He was chairman of the committee which reported a resolution to provide *a sinking fund* to pay the national debt, and which also reported the answer of Congress to the reasons of the Rhode-Island Legislature for rejecting the five per cent. impost. This answer (whoever may be its author) is excellent for the conclusiveness of its reasoning, and the moderation of its temper. We find him a member of another committee which made an interesting report on the non-compliance of the states with the requisitions of Congress, on the consequent failure of revenue, and on the necessity of vigorous and effectual measures to liquidate and fund the debt, and retrieve the credit of the nation. And he was one of the committee of three, which, in April, 1783, reported an address from Congress to the several states, calling upon them by all the motives of duty, interest, and gratitude, to vest Congress with the power to collect a general impost, as the only means by which they could discharge their sacred engagements. This address is distinguished for argument the most forcible, and eloquence the most impressive. And indeed the state papers generally of this interesting session, are models of composition, and specimens of research, of talents, of probity, and patriotism, which reflect the highest honour on our country. To deny to Mr. Hamilton his full share of agency in producing them, would be unjust, and I shall leave it to the good sense of every reader to draw their own conclusions from the facts which I have stated. It ought, however, to be recollected, that a member from Virginia, and who now fills the department of state, and who is well known and admired, if not for the energy, at least for the acuteness and elegance of his mind, was at this time an associated member with Gen. Hamilton in the business, and probably in the labours and honours of the session.

But there were other proceedings in that session which served to develope Mr. Hamilton's peculiar disposition and character. He was chairman of the committee which introduced a resolution full of gratitude for the disinterested and useful services of the Baron de Steuben; and he was the mover of the resolution for disbanding the army, and which was expressive of the well-founded confidence of Congress in the good sense and order of the troops, by allowing them a privilege, I believe totally unheard of before, *that they take their arms with them*. He appears also at that day to have entertained those sentiments which he, on a recent occasion, so eloquently enforced, respecting the full disclosure and free circulation of the *true* character and conduct of men in public trust, for he seconded the motion, stating, " *That it was of importance in every free country, that the conduct and sentiments of those to whom the direction of public affairs was committed, should be publicly known*, and that in future the doors of Congress ought to be opened, unless otherwise specially ordered."

AFTER the conclusion of this session of Congress, Mr. Hamilton returned to the practice of his profession, and soon drew to himself a general attention and applause, by his talents and eloquence at the Bar. His mind, however, was still directed to the progress and tendency of public measures. After the evacuation of New-York, the conduct of many of our citizens was intemperate and violent, and it gave currency to the pernicious doctrine, that the inhabitants of the southern district who had remained within the enemy's lines, were not entitled to the privileges of citizens, and that they were in fact *aliens*, subject to such penalties and disabilities as the legislature might, in their discretion, impose. To meet and overthrow this opinion, full of injustice and perfidy, and propagated under the influence of angry and malevolent passions, Mr. Hamilton published in the winter of 1784, his two pamphlets, under the signature of *Phocion*, and addressed to the considerate citizens of New-York. In these he stated, and recommended with ardour and with energy, the genuine obligations resulting from the treaty of peace; that no portion of our fellow-citizens were disfranchised, but that all were entitled to the full benefit of equal and impartial laws; that a perfidious evasion of the treaty, and measures of persecution and revenge, would disgrace the cause of liberty and the spirit of whigism, which was "generous, humane, beneficent, and just." These pamphlets carried with them universal conviction, and put the contrary opinion and the spirit it was enkindling, to disgrace and silence. The last pamphlet of Phocion is in a particular manner marked with that analysis of investigation; that deep basis of inquiry and logical deduction, which were peculiar to its illustrious author.

In 1786, Mr. Hamilton was chosen a member of Assembly for the city of New-York, and the ensuing session he brought forward a great measure, dictated by policy and patriotism, and which required his talents and firmness to maintain. I allude to the bill for acceding, on the part of this state, to the assumed independence of Vermont. We were then at an awful crisis in our national affairs, without a government to protect us, and just on the eve of a momentous experiment to effect one. Vermont was in fact independent, but she was not confederated; she was a stranger, and might soon become an enemy to the Union. This situation was delicate and alarming, and increased the anxieties of this great patriot, who then declared, in a speech unusually solemn and impressive, "That he was in the habit of viewing the situation of this country as replete with difficulties and surrounded with danger." The bill was opposed by counsel in behalf of such of our citizens as claimed lands within that jurisdiction. Mr. Hamilton, in a prompt and masterly manner, vindicated his proceeding, and showed that the state was under no obligation from the principles of the social compact, whatever they might choose to do from generosity or policy, to indemnify our citizens for losses sustained by a violent dismemberment of a part of the body politic, which they had not the power to prevent or reclaim. This speech, and the one in favour of the cession of the five per cent. impost to the United States, were models of senatorial argument and eloquence, which were greatly and justly admired at the time, and contributed in no small degree to his increasing fame and importance. In the last speech he took an enlarged view of the history and state of the Union, and undertook to demonstrate that there was no constitutional impediment to the adoption of the bill; that there was no danger to be apprehended to the public liberty from giving the power in question to the United States; that in the views of revenue the measure was indispensable, and that this country would soon be involved in misery and ruin, if our national affairs were left much longer to float in the chaos in which they were then involved. He at that time made a bold, frank, and affecting appeal to the uniform tenour of his life and character. " If in the public stations I have filled, I have acquitted myself with zeal, fidelity, and disinterestedness; if in the private walk of life my conduct has been unstained by any dishonourable act, I have a right to the confidence of those to whom I address myself."

During this session of our Legislature, Mr. Hamilton was chosen one of the three members to represent this state in the General Convention at Philadelphia, and he devoted the summer of 1787 to a faithful discharge of that important trust. A revolution in our national government was now at hand, and no man of strength and maturity, and whose breast was warmed with one spark of generous sensation, but felt for the perilous situation of the country, and contemplated with reverence the obligations it created. Mr. Hamilton was not of a nature to shrink from the crisis. He took a great and splendid share in the responsibilities of the day, and by writing, and speaking, and acting, he acquitted himself in a manner that ensured the admiration of his contemporaries, and will transmit his fame to posterity.

His particular services in the Convention are not accurately known to the public, as the doors of that body were closed, and their journals have never been published. I will take the liberty, however, of mentioning a remark once made by a very respectable member of the Convention from a neighbouring state, and leave those who can correct me to appreciate it as it may deserve. He said, that if the Constitution did not succeed on trial, Mr. Hamilton was less responsible for that result than any other member, for he fully and frankly pointed out to the Convention what he apprehended were the infirmities to which it was liable: And that if it answered the fond expectations of the public, the community would be more indebted to Mr. Hamilton than to any other member; for after its essential outlines were agreed to, he laboured the most indefatigably to heal those infirmities, and to guard against the evils to which they might expose it.

After the publication of the Constitution, Mr. Hamilton, in concert with Mr. Jay and Mr. Madison, commenced the *Federalist;* a series of Essays under the signature of *Publius*, addressed to the people of this state, in favour of the adoption of the Constitution. These papers first made their appearance in the daily prints early in November, 1787, and the work was not concluded until a short time previous to the meeting of the State Convention in June, 1788. It may be difficult to point out with precision the part that Mr. Hamilton took in the composition of these Essays.* It is, however, well understood, that Mr. Jay took but a very inconsiderable share in the work; that Mr. Madison took a deeper and more useful part, and that Mr. Hamilton was the principal author, and wrote at least three-fourths of the numbers. This work is not to be classed among those ephemeral productions which are calculated to produce a party purpose, and when that purpose is answered, to expire for ever. It is a profound and learned disquisition on the principles of a federal representative government, and combines equally an ardent attachment to public liberty, and an accurate discernment of the dangers resulting from an excessive jealousy of power, in those unsound and unskilful institutions, under which it has perished in almost every age and nation. This work will no doubt endure as long as any of the republican establishments of this country, on which it is such a luminous and elegant commentary. The first volume discusses these three interesting points — The utility of the union — The defects of the Confederation — And the necessity of a government as energetic, at least, as the one proposed; and this I regard as the most finished part of the work, considering the cogent and peculiarly affecting manner in which these propositions are surveyed, illustrated, and enforced. The Federalist was translated and published in France by *Buisson*, just as

* A key to the several writers is in our possession. — *Edit.*

that people were beginning to run the mad career of their revolution. It was spoken of in very high terms, although one of the Paris Gazettes thought some parts of it had rather *an aristocratical tendency*. Alas! for the cause of temperate and genuine liberty, if the leaders of that revolution had not been visionary philosophists, prostituted infidels, and blood-thirsty demagogues, the mild light of this western star might possibly have rescued that people from the tempestuous fury of the passions; from a constant vibration between scenes of folly, and scenes of horror, and conducted them to peace, liberty, and safety. I am happy to find that a new edition of this invaluable work has lately appeared, in a very handsome style, from the press of Mr. Hopkins, in New-York. It ought to be taught in our schools, and studied by our lawyers and statesmen, as an elementary code of instruction and wisdom.

Mr. Hamilton was a member of the State Convention, which met in the summer of 1788, and he was there actively employed for six weeks in enforcing, by his eloquent speeches, the principles he had previously, and so much at large, detailed in the Federalist. The sketch of the debates which was published, conveyed a very inadequate idea of the talents and arguments employed in the mutual discussions which took place in that assembly. The speeches of Mr. Hamilton, which I should select as containing the best display of his sound and pre-eminent mind, were those in vindication of the constitutional stability and permanency of the Senate of the United States. In these he undertook to demonstrate that the organization of that branch ought to be as strong, at least, as they found it; and that from the nature of man and the lessons of experience, it was to be seen that a firm, stable body in the government, was essential to correct the prejudices, check the passions, and control the fluctuations of the more popular branch.

THE constitution having gone into operation, and the executive departments being established, Mr. Hamilton was appointed, in the summer of 1789, to the office of Secretary of the Treasury. This office he held between five and six years; and when we look back to the measures that, within that period, he originated, matured, and vindicated, we are astonished in the contemplation of the various powers of his vigorous and exalted mind. His *reports* were so many didactic dissertations, laboriously wrought and highly finished, on some of the most intricate and abstract subjects in political economy. Among those reports we designate as the most interesting, his report of January, 1790, on a provision for the support of the public credit; of December, 1790, on the establishment of a national bank; of December, 1791, on the subject of manufactures; and of January, 1795, (being his last official act) on a plan for the further support of public credit. Mr. Hamilton may justly be regarded as the *Founder of the Public Credit* of this country. He raised it from the dust, and placed it on sound foundations. His great moving principle of action in his department, was *good faith* —was a punctual performance of contracts. And that the national credit might be placed beyond the reach of any stroke that could in the least degree annoy or alarm it, he urged to Congress the express renunciation, by law, of all right to tax the public funds, or to sequester at any time, or on any pretext, the property of foreigners therein. He enabled this country to know, feel, and develope its immense resources, and under his administration, the finances advanced to a state of prosperity beyond all expectation, and so as to engage the attention and command the confidence of Europe. And so far from giving colour to the vile calumny which has been insinuated against him, that he patronized the doctrine that *a public debt was a public blessing*, he inculcates with great solicitude in his reports, that the progressive accumulation of debt was the natural *disease* of all governments; that it ought to be guarded against with provident foresight and inflexible perseverance; that it ought to be a fundamental maxim in the system of public credit, (and which he uniformly endeavoured to enforce by practice); *that the creation of debt should always be accompanied with the means of extinguishment;* that the observance of this axiom was the true secret to render public credit immortal. In his last report, he recommends a provision for augmenting the *sinking fund*, so as to render it commensurate with the entire debt of the United States; and he proposed to secure that fund by a sanction the most inviolable, and which was no less than to make the application of the fund to the object, *a part of the contract with the creditor*. By such means, and with such efforts, did he build up and establish the important interests of the nation confided to his care: he has left to his successors little more to do than to follow his precepts, and to shine by the lustre of his example.

His report on manufactures is a *chef d'œuvre* of the kind, and the most laboured performance that he ever gave to the world. It is not more distinguished for knowledge and investigation, than for having given a deep wound to the tenets of the sect of the French *economists*, and also to another system of politics which had grown fashionable among political philosophers. The system I allude to, is to be met with in *Smith's*

Inquiry into the Wealth of Nations. This report adopts the principles of the mercantile system, and leaves the theory of Smith as amusing and beautiful in speculation, but which, in the present state of things, is not reducible to practice. That bold, profound, and systematic writer, who attacked the manufacturing and mercantile interests of Great Britain as founded upon an oppressive monopoly, lays down an entire freedom of commerce and industry, undiverted and unimpeded by government, as the best means of advancing nations to prosperity and greatness. The secretary combats with great ability some of the fundamental principles of this doctrine, and he adopts the mercantile system upon the basis of self-defence, and as most wise, because Europe perseveres in the same system.

All his principal reports are remarkable for uniting depth of research with clearness of perception, the closest logic with the utmost purity and precision of expression; and his official labours in this department, united with the honesty with which he conducted it, and which the most penetrating inquisition into all the avenues of his office could never question, will, perhaps, form with posterity the fairest monument of his fame.

Mr. Hamilton, in his character of Secretary of the Treasury, was also one of the constitutional advisers of the President in relation generally to the duties of his office, and I apprehend that few, if any matters of moment, were transacted without the sanction of his counsel. The season during which he presided over the treasury department, was unusually critical. The French revolution progressed with a rapidity and violence that threatened to involve the whole civilized world in combustion and ruin. Not content with their own regeneration, the French rulers, in 1793, adopted the intolerance of the Koran, and began to propagate their new faith by the sword, and to carry on an universal war, either of force or of fraud, against all the unbelieving nations of the earth, and against all the governments under which they lived, as being so many monuments of tyranny and superstition. At this awful crisis, a furious war is begun against Great Britain, and M. Genet is sent as minister to the United States, charged with secret instructions (which he afterwards published, and on which he faithfully acted) to *excite the Americans*, even if their ministers should be *timid and wavering*, to make a *common cause with France* in the new war she had then commenced. To meet this important epoch, the Proclamation of Neutrality was issued by the President of the United States; and to defend that great measure as lawful and expedient, against the prejudices and passions which the French minister had but too successfully excited, the essays of *Pacificus* appeared.

These essays were written and published by Mr. Hamilton in the summer of 1793; and of all his productions, none ever appeared at a more seasonable juncture, or were calculated to produce a more auspicious effect. Their object was to prove that the President had competent authority to issue the proclamation in question:—That it was only a declaration of what was the existing law of the land, the neutrality of our government, and that as constitutional executor of the laws, it would be his duty to see that neutrality faithfully observed:—That we were under no obligation from existing treaties to become a party in the war:—That, considering the peculiar origin and nature of the warfare, the United States had valid and honourable pleas against any interference:—That the obligations of gratitude imposed upon nations the mutual returns of good-will and benevolence, but were no sufficient ground for war; and that those obligations would more naturally point to the hand from whom antecedent favours had been received, and which, in this case, was the amiable and unfortunate monarch whom the revolution had just swept from the throne.

It cannot be denied that these essays were too well written, and addressed themselves too powerfully to the interest and good sense of the country, not to have had their influence in rendering popular this important act of administration; and it is well known that the proclamation received afterwards the sanction not only of Congress, but of the community at large.

In January, 1795, Mr. Hamilton resigned the office of Secretary of the Treasury, and once more returned to private life. But he still felt himself charged to vindicate another important measure of the government, of which he had no doubt been a responsible adviser; I allude to Mr. Jay's negociation and treaty with Great-Britain. This treaty had to encounter inveterate prejudices and combustible materials, which spread their root as far back as the revolutionary war, but which had been enkindled and armed with tenfold virulence by the pestilential breath of the French Revolution. Even at this late day, the temperate historian is admonished to tread lightly over these ashes of party-spirit. Mr. Hamilton devoted the summer of 1795 to a defence of this treaty, in a series of Essays under the signature of *Camillus*. The first twenty-two numbers were appropriated to an examination of the ten permanent articles of this treaty, and which articles continue to this day the law of the land. The remainder of the treaty was commercial and temporary, and has already expired. The discussion of this latter part was not equal in interest, and being written with less attention, and by different hands, was not equal in ability to the other. But this defence, taken together, must now be considered by every competent and impartial reader, as one of the most full and satisfactory illustrations that perhaps ever was given of a complicated diplomatic question. I presume there does not exist any thing among the piles of European state papers, to be compared to it; although one reason for this may be, that in Europe no such precise and *formal* vindication of any national treaty, has ever been deemed requisite. The beneficial effects of this treaty, and which are known and felt constantly, have at last accomplished what argument alone could not do — they have forced an universal conviction upon the public mind; and all the dead spectres which were conjured up at the time to terrify the imagination, and blind the judgment, have long since disappeared before the light of experience. It is to be observed that the question was not whether the treaty was in all respects the most desirable, (for treaties are acts of *mutual* accommodation) but the true question was, whether the treaty did not adjust, in a reasonable manner, the points in controversy between the two nations; and whether our interests did not demand, and our honour permit us to adopt it. The sanction it received from our government, and the general approbation it has ultimately met with, overcoming in its progress the stream of prejudice, and the obstacles of foreign intrigue and menace, have given the definitive answer to this question. The articles upon which Camillus more emphatically bent and exhausted the strength and resources of his mind, were the 3d article, on the intercourse between the United States and Canada; and the 10th article, providing against the confiscation of private debts in time of war. I beg leave to recommend these two heads of his performance as uncommonly excellent. The latter is a finished treatise by itself, and forms a chapter on the law of nations, equally accurate, didactic, and moral. It vindicates the treaty-stipulation on the ground of reason and principle, of policy and expediency, on the opinions of the most enlightened jurists, and the usage of nations.

The last great occasion which called Mr. Hamilton forward upon the theatre of public action, existed in the spring of the year 1798. It will be recollected that France had been long making piratical depredations upon our commerce; that negociation and a pacific adjustment had been repeatedly attempted on the part of this country, without success; that our minister had been refused an audience; that three ministers extraordinary had been treated with the grossest indignity, and money demanded of the United States on terms the most degrading. The doors of reconciliation being thus barred, we had no honourable alternative left, but open and determined resistance.

And what was the power that had thus used us? It was a power the most terrible in strength; the most daring in project; the most unchecked in means; the most fatal to its victims, of any that a righteous providence had hitherto permitted to exist upon this globe, for the awful chastisement of the human race. All the States, even of the republican form, that fell within her widespread grasp; the United Netherlands, Geneva, the Swiss Cantons, Genoa, and Venice, had already been prostrated by her arms, or her still more formidable caresses. She was at that moment busy in her schemes of universal domination, and was fitting out a vast armament in the ports of the Mediterranean, for some distant expedition of conquest and plunder. At this portentous period, Mr. Hamilton published *The Stand*, or a series of essays under the signature of *Titus Manlius*, with a view to rouse the people of this country to a sense of their impending danger, and to measures of defence, which should be at once vigorous and manly.

In these Essays he portrays, with the glow and colouring of a master-artist, the conduct of revolutionizing France towards her own people and towards other nations, and he shows that she had undermined the main pillars of civilized society; that she betrayed a plan to disorganize the human mind itself, by attempting to destroy all religious opinion, and pervert a whole people to atheism; that her ruling passions were ambition and fanaticism, and that she aimed equally to proselyte, subjugate, and debase every government without distinction, to effect the aggrandizement of the "Great Nation"! He then gave a detail of the accumulated injuries and insults we had received from France, and showed that her object was to degrade and humble our government, and prepare the way for revolution and conquest. He concluded, as the result of his work, that we ought to suspend our treaties with France, fortify our harbours, defend our commerce on the ocean, attack their predatory cruisers on our coast, create a respectable naval force, and raise, or organize and discipline, a considerable army, as an indispensable precaution against attempts at invasion, which might put in jeopardy our very existence as a nation. He considered that militia alone would be a very inadequate and fallacious reliance against veteran troops, headed by some enterprising chief; but that when we had made the defensive preparations he had recommended, we could then meet their aggressions in the attitude of calm defiance.

So undeniable were all these facts, so irresistible were the conclusions which he drew from them, that in the summer of 1798, these measures suggested by Mr. Hamilton were all literally carried into execution by Congress, and received the warm and hearty sanction of the nation. An honourable, proud, and manly sentiment, was then enkindled and pervaded the continent; it reflected high honour on our national character, and that character was transmitted to Europe, as a means of respect and a pledge of security.

A NEW provisional army, consisting, however, of but twelve regiments of infantry, and six troops of light dragoons, was ordered to be immediately raised, and Mr. Hamilton, upon the express and pointed solicitations of General Washington, was appointed *Inspector-General.* On the death of that great man, he succeeded to the office of *Commander in Chief*, and continued in that character for a few months, and until this little army was disbanded in the summer of 1800.

DURING this military avocation, Gen. Hamilton bestowed indefatigable efforts to organize and discipline the troops; and he improved himself greatly in the study of the science of war, and of the kindred sciences of mathematics, geometry, and chemistry, of which he was particularly fond. And should any crisis have arisen, in the future destinies of our country, in which some hero or statesman would have been wanted "in resisting mischief, or effecting good," the eyes of America would no doubt have been concentrated on this first and fairest of her sons. But alas! these dreams of consolation are gone! He has fallen by the hands of a *base assassin!* — Accept, venerable shade, this tribute of a friend, who regards thy loss as a great national calamity, and recollects thy talents and virtues with the purest respect, and the fondest devotion!

The Albany Centinel of August 29, presents us with the following affecting article:

"Incidental circumstances have prevented our noticing, of late, many passing occurrences of the day, as they deserve. One of these, and which we consider by no means the least interesting, is the manner in which our Supreme Court testified their respect for the character of Gen. Hamilton, and deep affliction for his death, at their session in this city, which closed on the 18th inst. By direction of the judges, the bench, the bar, including the seats of the counsellors and attornies, the clerk's desk and table, and the wall back of the judges' seat, were hung in black during the term.* In no place, perhaps, could a tribute of this kind have been offered with a more striking effect. It is here, more than any where, that all who have attended court, with whatever motive, feel the deprivation of its late *peerless* member. It is here we recollect our first inquiries used to be, as if every grati-

* The same mark of respect was paid to his memory by the Mayor's Court in this city, where Mr. Clinton presides.

fication depended upon it, is Hamilton in town? and if present, his engaging address and his intelligent eye never failed to interest us — to raise our expectations. — " When he began, we were attentive — an harmonious voice — select expressions — elevated sentiment. He divided his subject — we perceived his distinctions : nothing perplexed — nothing insipid — nothing languid. He unfolded the web of his argument — we were enthralled. He refuted the sophism — we were freed. He introduced a pertinent narrative — we were interested. He modulated his voice — we were charmed. He was jocular — we smiled. He pressed serious truths — we yielded to their force. He addressed the passions — the tears glided down our cheeks. And had he raised his voice in anger, we should have trembled and wished ourselves away." Here, and in him, have we often seen the human character raised to its "noon-tide point." Alas! how chilling is this sable contrast!"

Who can read, without heartfelt emotion, the subsequent Communication, from the same paper?

"*Communication.* — On Sunday morning the afflicted Mrs. Hamilton attended divine service in the Presbyterian Church in this city, with her three little sons.

"At the close of a prayer by the Rev. Mr. Nott, the eldest dropped on his face, in a fainting fit.

"Two gentlemen immediately raised him, and while bearing him out of the church, the afflicted mother sprung forward, in the agonies of grief and despair, towards her apparently lifeless son.

"The heart-rending scenes she had recently struggled

with, called forth all the fine-spun sensibilities of her nature — and seemed to say, that nature must, and will be indulged in her keenest sorrows — She was overpowered in the conflict, and likewise sunk — uttering such heart-rending groans, and inward sighs, as would have melted into mingled sympathies, even Burr himself.

" BOTH of them soon recovered — and while the little son was supported standing on the steps, yet speechless, the most affecting scene presented itself — a scene, could it be placed on canvas by the hand of a master, would be in the highest degree interesting and impressive. The mother, in this tender situation, fastened herself upon the son, with her head reclining on his left shoulder — the agonies so strongly painted on her countenance — her long flowing weeds — the majesty of her person — the position of both — and above all, the peculiarity of their trying situation in the recent loss of a husband, and a father — who could refrain from invoking on the head of the guilty author of their miseries, those curses he so rightly merits? The curse of living despised, and execrated by the voice of a whole nation — the curse of being held up to the view of future ages — a MONSTER, and an ASSASSIN."

THE following pious extract from a late Sermon, delivered in the northern part of this state, is well calculated to produce the most salutary effect.

FROM THE LANSINGBURGH GAZETTE.

EXTRACT from a Sermon on the death of General Hamilton, delivered in this village, by the Rev. Mr. Blatchford, on Sunday, the 22d ult.

*****" Again — Is not a preparation for death and eternity a part of true honour? And what if thou shouldst thyself fall in the contest? How dreadful are the consequences! A state of horror, distraction, malice, revenge, remorse: Torn in a moment from all the delights of life, and all the advantages of a time of probation for eternity. Is this the temper which becomes a dying hour? That hour we all would wish tranquil and serene; undisturbed by passion, unagitated by care: full of penitence, humility, gratitude, and submission that we may meditate the awful change, and resign with composure our parting souls into the hands of the creator. Alas! how different is this from that scene of frenzy we have been contemplating! but how much is the interest of these remarks increased by the intimation of Eternity! Remember, O man! that the soul which now animates thy frame, is destined to survive the pang of dissolution. — Allow me, therefore, to reason with thee a little before thou committest the act of madness. Pause — Ponder — Where art thou? Whither art thou going? What mayest thou soon be? Thou art about to launch into that awful ocean, whose domains are unbounded and unknown! Thou art standing upon the very brink of eternity. Eternity! what art thou? Our faculties are lost in the contemplation of thee. We soar; we stretch; but all is dark beyond! No one is permitted to return and bring us tidings of thee! Yet let us not be presumptuously inquisitive. A short time hence, and we shall explore thy vast dominions. We then shall know *what it is to die*. But O! thou all wise disposer, forbid that the solemn hour shall find us unprepared, much less that we should accelerate its approach. No: " All the days of my appointed time will I wait, till my change come!" Thou rash adventurer! let conscience speak.

Hold thy impious hand. — Forbear a crime at which thy heart recoils; which thy reason condemns; which christianity has accursed; at which angels weep, the devils triumph, and to punish which, the red flaming sword of justice is for ever unsheathed.

"But supposing thou shouldst survive, and be the means of the death of the man whose ruin thou didst predetermine: We then proceed to ask, Is it not honourable to prevent distress; to sooth the tender heart, ready to break for anguish; to heal the wounds of the widow's soul, and dry up the tears of the orphan; to secure to thy country, talents which dazzle by their lustre, and in their exertion have an irresistible and commanding influence? Thy act then must be stamped with the deepest turpitude, and be sealed with the broadest mark of infamy. Perhaps thine antagonist, whom thou hast drawn into the field, is the father of a numerous family, and the husband of an affectionate wife. Methinks I see the disconsolate widow, which thou hast made, wringing her hands in anguish, and pouring out her soul in unavailing tears. Thou hast plunged a dagger into a heart that never offended thee. O desperate ruffian! Didst thou not reflect upon the barbarous deed? Was there nothing in female helplessness, widowed and alone, to stay thine hand? But O! what sight is here — here are seven lovely children, and one of them an infant! Thou hast made them orphans, and left them to a precarious fate. Dost thou not hear their distressful cries? Dost thou not see their gushing tears? Thou hast left them unprotected, in a dangerous world, and rudely deprived them of the tender hand, which might have led them to virtue and to usefulness. They cry in vain upon their sire.

Thou hast sent him to the silent tomb, and they shall see his face no more. But perhaps thou hast stained thine hands with the blood of a patriot, whose uncommon genius was exerted in early life to save that country which gave thee birth, and which thou art bound to respect by the most solemn and imposing obligations. Was there nothing in the fair character of his honour to restrain the weapon of destruction? Did you not reflect upon his well-earned fame; or was it envy of his greatness which prompted the savage deed? Did you not think upon a country in tears; and in the impulse of veneration universally to be paid to the memory of the departed hero, hear the execration of thy act?— But perhaps he stood high in professional merit, and his eloquence and his knowledge gave him the first place in public admiration and distinction! Was there nothing in his illustrious talents to soften thy spirit and make thee distrust thy own rashness? No, nothing in this, nor in any of these, to restrain thy fury. Thou hast accomplished the fatal purpose. Thou hast mocked the tears of the widow; neglected the cries of the orphans; injured thy country in the death of her magnanimous friend; and stifled eloquence and genius, in the destruction of their favourite son!— My brethren! this is not a fancied picture— for *Hamilton* is slain! He who was the associate of your beloved Washington; and as he himself expresses it, " *his principal, and most confidential aid; whose acknowledged abilities and integrity placed him on high ground; and made him a conspicuous character in the United States, and even in Europe,*" is slain! He is no more, of whom the father of your country declared, that " *his ambition was of that laudable kind, which prompts a man to excel in whatever he takes in hand; who was enterprising, quick in his perceptions, and in his judgment intuitively great.**" Will you not, my brethren, deeply regret the cause of his death, whilst you mourn the death itself!"

The following proceedings of the Cincinnati, at Charleston, will be read with uncommon interest by every good man, and we hope be followed by a similar measure here and elsewhere.

FROM THE CHARLESTON COURIER.

Mr. Editor,

Please to insert in your paper, for the information of the public, the following circular letter and memorial, which have been agreed upon by the joint committee of the State-Society of Cincinnati, and of the American Revolution Society, in pursuance of resolutions adopted by these Societies.

Charleston, S. C. September 12, 1804.
Sir,

Having been appointed by the South-Carolina State Society of the Cincinnati, and the American Revolution Society, a joint committee for draughting and circulating a memorial to the Legislature, praying for legislative interference to restrain the practice of *duelling*, we have agreed on the enclosed memorial, and transmit it to you, with our earnest request that you would use your most vigorous exertions to have it generally signed. It is unnecessary to dilate on the mischievous consequences of Duelling, to induce your endeavours to check a practice so dishonourable to this state, in which it is our boast to

* Vide Washington's letter to President Adams, recommending Gen. Hamilton as second in command, in the late army of the United States.

be governed by laws, and not by men. The necessity of applying to the Legislature on the subject, is obvious; for it is well known, that the existing laws have never brought any Duellist to serious inconveniences, and there is well founded reason for believing that they never can, in consequence of the weight of precedents to the contrary. Our only alternative, therefore, is to acquiesce in the practice of Duelling, or to restrain it by a new law. The difficulties of framing any law, that may afford an adequate remedy to the evil, are great, but not insurmountable.

It is not to be supposed that our Legislature is less wise than that of several of our sister states, whose laws have been so operative that in several of them, *duels* are absolutely unknown. If a respectable number of the friends of good government, morality, and religion, sign the memorial we have forwarded, or any similar one, the Legislature, ever attentive to the wishes of their constituents, will enter seriously on the business, and we doubt not of their *ability* to frame such regulations as will certainly abolish the evil.

Independent of any law which may be passed, the sentiments of the most respectable part of the community, in opposition to *duelling*, declared and avowed by signing the memorial, will have a very beneficial effect. It will tend to correct the public opinion, and to restrain all who wish for the esteem of their fellow-citizens, from engaging in a practice which the virtue and good sense of the community have so pointedly denounced. These, and many other arguments, which must occur on reflection, will be sufficient to convince you, that in procuring signers to the memorial, you will do a service acceptable to God and beneficial to man. We have further to request you, to forward the memorial to Columbia, by the first Monday in November next, that they may all be presented together to the Legislature on the first day of their meeting; when we hope for the sublime pleasure of seeing an abhorrence of duelling pointedly expressed by many thousands of our most deserving citizens.

  We are, with great respect,
    Your most obedient servants,
  CHARLES C. PINCKNEY, JAMES KENNEDY, WILLIAM READ, Committee of the Cincinnati. DAVID RAMSAY, HENRY W. DESAUSSURE, WILLIAM ALLEN DEAS, JAMES LOWNDES, RICHARD FURMAN, Committee of the American Revolution Society.

  P. S. IMPRESSED with a firm belief that many advantages would result from illuminating the public mind on the inconsistency of the spirit and principles of the practice against which the memorial is levelled, with the spirit and principles of our holy religion, we earnestly request, as a particular favour, that you would, at some convenient early day, preach a sermon on the sin and folly of *Duelling*. When the public sentiment is correctly made up on this subject, the advocates for duelling will be struck with their inconsistency, in claiming for themselves the high and honourable appellation of Christians. In our opinion, public previous notice of the day on which the proposed sermon will be preached, would, in general, be both proper and useful; but, on this subject, you will judge for yourself.

  N. B. THE above postscript is omitted in all letters which are not addressed to Clergymen.

To the Honourable the President and Members of the Senate, and the Honourable the Speaker, and the other Members of the House of Representatives of the State of South-Carolina.

The Memorial of the Subscribers, Citizens of the said State,
SHOWETH,

THAT your memorialists are deeply impressed with grief at the prevalence of the custom of *duelling*, which, trampling upon all laws, human and divine, sweeps off many useful citizens, leaving their families a prey to sorrow, and often to poverty and vice.

THAT this custom originated in dark and barbarous ages, when a regular and impartial administration of justice was unknown and unpractised — but it ought not to be tolerated by the civilization of modern times, under a legislation which has provided, or may easily provide, adequate redress, for all serious injuries committed against the life, liberty, fame, or property of the citizen.

THAT this custom erects a tribunal for the settlement of personal differences, in which, contrary to all sound principles, a man becomes the sole judge in his own cause; whence, as might have been expected from such a code, the only punishments for the lowest, as well as highest offences, are written in blood.

THAT restraining personal resentments, by giving the attribute of vengeance to the laws, was the greatest victory obtained by civilization over barbarism — but the custom of *duelling* is too well calculated to defeat the beneficial effects of that triumph, and to weaken the authority of all laws, by accustoming men to contemn their sanctions.

THAT your memorialists are apprehensive from the frequency of the practice of late years, that this custom is gaining ground, and seems likely to be carried to such great lengths, as to degrade men to the condition of gladiators, and to introduce anew the reign of barbarism.

THAT from the nature of the human mind, men are ever ready to follow examples, especially those set by eminent persons; when, therefore, the body of the community perceives great, and in other respects virtuous citizens, shedding each other's blood on slight provocations, or trivial pretences, the fatal practice becomes general. Thus the barriers between virtue and vice, innocence and guilt, are broken down; and that horror of shedding human blood wantonly, which is the best safeguard of the peace of society, is greatly diminished, or wholly destroyed.

THAT in countries where distinctions of rank are sanctioned, a pernicious custom may exist, and be confined to the higher orders of society, and be, comparatively, little destructive — but that, in our country of equal laws, rights, and rank, such custom, if unchecked by the laws, will necessarily become general, and spread its destructive effects far and wide in the community, to the desolation of thousands of families.

THAT this mortal vengeance is not resorted to merely in cases of grievous injuries, for which the laws may not have provided an adequate remedy: but in many cases of trivial offence, which a generous mind would willingly pardon, this tyrant custom is supposed to impose an obligation, to call out to the field of blood even a companion or friend, who may have unguardedly given the provocation.

THAT this absurd custom decides no right, and settles no point; as the religion and philosophy of modern times will not admit, that the Almighty Disposer of events will interpose his power on such an impious appeal to his justice; which the credulity of the Gothic nations believed, when this custom existed among them, in the form of judicial combat. It is, therefore, conceded universally, that the innocent and aggrieved person is as likely to be the victim, as the guilty offender, and probably more so, as a mild and peaceable man would be less inclined to acquire or exert a murderous skill, the effect of which he abhors.

THAT the pretence of those who would excuse this custom, on the ground that it polishes society, and prevents assassination, is wholly unfounded: as the most polished nations of ancient times, the Grecians and Romans; and the most humane and civilized nation of modern times, the Chinese, have enjoyed society in perfection, without the adventitious aid of this pernicious and unnatural custom; which though in direct hostility to the principles of christianity, prevails only in Christian Europe and America.

YOUR memorialists have been informed, that although the common law of the land declares homicide in a duel, to be murder, the law has become obsolete, and a dead letter — That all the decisions in our courts of justice, have turned wholly on the fairness with which the duel was conducted; and verdicts of acquittal, or of manslaughter, have constantly been rendered — thence arises a necessity for a clear and explicit expression of the legislative will, on this important subject, guaranteed by new and vigorous sanctions.

Your memorialists, therefore, humbly pray that your honourable house would be pleased to take this important subject into your most serious consideration; and that you would, in your wisdom, provide such remedies as may, effectually, destroy the evil practice complained of, by regulations, wisely calculated to protect the fame and feelings of the innocent and insulted person; and to punish, rigorously, the bold offender who shall dare to lift his hand against his neighbour, and shed his blood in a duel, in violation of the divine law and the law of his country.

We suspect the following affectionate tribute of the Scottish Muse, which is taken from a paper in the county of Washington, state of Pennsylvania, is from the well known pen of Mr. Bruce, whose little volume of poetry has, not long since, been perused by us with high admiration.

FROM THE WESTERN TELEGRAPHE.

General Hamilton having been a member of the St. Andrew's Society of the city of New-York, the following verses will not be unacceptable to the members of that Society throughout the union, particularly to such of them as are native Scotsmen.

The subject undoubtedly claims a much higher species

of Poetry; but there is none in which the simple and genuine feelings of nature can be so happily expressed as that which I have adopted.

ON THE
MURDER OF HAMILTON.

A SCOTCH BALLAD.

Tune — " *Good night, and joy be wi' ye a'!* "

OH! wo betide ye, Aaron Burr!
    May mickle curse upo' ye fa'!
Ye 've kill'd as brave a gentleman
    As e'er liv'd in America.

Wi' bloody mind ye ca'd him out,
    Wi' practis'd e'e did on him draw,
And wi' deliberate, murderous aim,
    Ye kill'd the flower o' America.

A nobler heart, an abler head,
    Nor this, nor any nation saw;
He was his Country's hope and pride,
    The darling of America.

Wha now, like him, wi' temper'd fire,
    His country's "sword will strongly draw;"
And, mid the furious onset, spare
    The vanquish'd foes o' America?

Wha now, like him, wi' honest zeal,
    Will argue in the Senate ha',
And 'lighten wi' his genius' rays,
    The interests of America?

Mild, mild was he, o' tenderest heart,
    Kind and sincere without a flaw;
A loving husband, father, friend;
    And oh! he lov'd America.

Torn by a murderer's desperate arm,
    Frae midst his friends and family a',
  He's gone — the first of men is gone —
    The Glory of America!

  Where'er ye go, O! Aaron Burr!
    The worm of conscience ay will gnaw;
  Your haunted fancy ay will paint
    Your bloody deed in America.

  But though ye flee o'er land and sea,
    And 'scape your injur'd country's law,
  The red right hand of angry Heaven
    Will yet avenge America.

  O save us, Heaven! frae faction's rage;
    Our headstrong passions keep in awe!
  And frae ambition's hidden arts,
    O God! preserve America.

THE following highly finished "Sketch," as the author modestly calls it, is taken from the Boston Repertory, the leading federal print of New-England. We have no hesitation in pronouncing this "Sketch," take it together, equal, at least, to anything we have on record from the pen of Edmund Burke, whose charming manner it so closely resembles; nor is it surpassed by the celebrated character of Chatham by Grattan. Yet must it be owned that it is not uniformly excellent. We mean not to enter into criticism in detail, but, in our opinion, the manner in which allusion is made to Greece and Rome, is tame and beneath the rest of the piece. Instead of saying, "Such a patriot, the best Romans in their best days would have admitted to *citizenship* and the consulate;" and that "the name of Hamilton would not have dishonoured Greece in the age of Aristides," would it not have been much nearer the truth, and more like the rest of the sketch, to have said, that had either Greece or Rome ever possessed a citizen who concentrated in himself such vast talents, such disinterested patriotism, so many private virtues, so many amiable qualities, and who had from the purest motives, rendered his country such invaluable services as Alexander Hamilton, it would have added a greater lustre to the fortunate country who could have claimed the honour of giving birth to such a prodigy, than the annals of either can now boast of? The concluding sentence is, also, in our judgment, a little inconsistent with what has preceded, and a falling off.

The editor of that paper thus refers his readers to this eminently beautiful picture — " Reader, do you wish to regale your mind, your taste, your sensibility? Then turn to the first page. Are you curious to know who has furnished you such a repast? He whose writings have long given character, as they have given intelligence, to New-England.*"

FROM THE BOSTON REPERTORY.

The following Sketch was prepared, immediately after the death of the ever to be lamented HAMILTON, and was lately read to a select company of friends, at whose desire it is published.

There are so many persons, who, from various causes, possess only a superficial knowledge of the character of eminent men, that it is to be expected the extraordinary marks of grief manifested by the public, on the death of General Hamilton, will to some appear strange, and to others excessive. America, they may say, has produced many great men; some are dead, and others remain

* Supposed to be the Honourable Fisher Ames.

alive. Why then should we mourn, as if with a sense of desolation and surprise, for a loss, that by the lot of human nature, has already become familiar, and why mourn so much, as if all was lost, when we have so many great men left?

BUT although General Hamilton has, for some years, withdrawn from public office to the bar, and has been, in some measure, out of the view and contemplation of his countrymen, there was nevertheless a splendour in his character that could not be contracted within the ordinary sphere of his employments.

IT is with really great men, as with great literary works, the excellence of both is best tested by the extent and durableness of their impression. The public has not suddenly, but after an experience of five-and-twenty years, taken that impression of the just celebrity of Alexander Hamilton, which nothing but his extraordinary intrinsic merit could have made, and still less could have made so deep, and maintained so long. In this case, it is safe and correct to judge by effects. We sometimes calculate the height of a mountain, by measuring the length of its shadow.

IT is not a party, for party distinctions, to the honour of our citizens, be it said, are confounded by the event; it is a nation that weeps for its bereavement. We weep as the Romans did over the ashes of Germanicus. It is a thoughtful, foreboding sorrow, that takes possession of the heart, and sinks it with no counterfeited heaviness.

IT is here proper, and not invidious, to remark, that as the emulation excited by conducting great affairs, commonly trains and exhibits great talents, it is seldom the case that the fairest and soundest judgment of a great man's merit, is to be gained, exclusively, from his associates in counsel or action. Persons of conspicuous merit themselves are, not unfrequently, bad judges, and still worse witnesses on this point: often rivals, sometimes enemies, almost always unjust, and still oftener envious or cold; the opinions they give to the public, as well as those they privately form for themselves, are, of course, discoloured with the hue of their prejudices and resentments.

But the body of the people, who cannot feel a spirit of rivalship towards those whom they see elevated by nature and education so far above their heads, are more equitable, and, supposing a competent time and opportunity for information on the subject, more intelligent judges. Even party rancour, eager to maim the living, scorns to strip the slain. The most hostile passions are soothed or baffled by the fall of their antagonist. Then, if not sooner, the very multitude will fairly decide on character, according to their experience of its impression; and as long as virtue, not unfrequently for a time obscured, is ever respectable when distinctly seen, they cannot withhold, and they will not stint their admiration.

If then the popular estimation is ever to be taken for the true one, the uncommonly profound public sorrow for the death of Alexander Hamilton, sufficiently explains and vindicates itself. He had not made himself dear to the passions of the multitude, by condescending, in defiance of his honour and conscience, to become their instrument. He is not lamented because a skilful flatterer is now mute for ever. It was by the practice of no art, by wearing no disguise, it was not by accident, nor by the levity nor profligacy of party, but in despite of its malignant misrepresentation, it was by bold and inflexible adherence to truth, by loving his country better than himself, preferring its interest to its favour, and serving it, when it was unwilling and unthankful, in a manner that no other person could, that he rose; and the *true* popularity, the homage that is paid to virtue, followed him. It was not in the power of party or envy to pull him down, but he rose, as if some force of attraction drew him to the skies. He rose, and the very prejudice that could not reach, was at length almost ready to adore him.

It is indeed no imagined wound that inflicts so keen an anguish. Since the news of his death, the novel and strange events of Europe have succeeded each other unregarded, the nation has been enchained to its subject, and broods over its grief, which is more deep than eloquent; which, though dumb, can make itself felt without utterance, and which does not merely pass, but, like an electrical shock, at the same instant smites and astonishes, as it passes from Georgia to Newhampshire.

There is a kind of force put upon our thoughts by this disaster that detains and rivets them to a closer contemplation of those resplendent virtues that are now lost, except to memory, and there they will dwell for ever.

That writer would deserve the fame of a public benefactor, who could exhibit the character of Hamilton with the truth and force that all who intimately knew him conceived it; his example would then take the same ascendant as his talents. The portrait alone, however exquisitely finished, could not inspire genius where it is not; but if the world should again have possession of so rare a gift, it might awaken it where it sleeps, as by a spark from heaven's own altar: for, surely, if there is any thing like divinity in man, it is in his admiration of virtue.

But who alive can exhibit this portrait? If our age, on that supposition more fruitful than any other, had produced two Hamiltons, one of them might then have depicted the other. To delineate genius one must feel its power. Hamilton, and he alone, with all its inspiration, could have transfused its whole fervid soul into the picture, and swelled its lineaments into life. The writer's mind, expanding with his own enthusiasm, and glowing with kindred fires, would then have stretched to the dimensions of his subject.

Such is the infirmity of human nature, it is very difficult for a man, who is greatly the superior of his associates, to preserve their friendship without abatement. Yet though Hamilton could not possibly conceal his superiority, he was so little inclined to display it, he was so much at ease in its possession, that no jealousy or envy chilled his bosom when his friends obtained praise: he was indeed, so entirely the friend of his friends, so magnanimous, so superior, or more properly, so insensible to all exclusive selfishness of spirit, so frank, so ardent, yet so little overbearing, so much trusted, admired, beloved, almost adored, that his power over their affections was entire and lasted through his life. We do not believe that he left any worthy man his foe who had ever been his friend. Men of the most elevated minds have not always the readiest discernment of character. Perhaps he was sometimes too sudden and too lavish in bestowing his confidence: his manly spirit, disdaining artifice, suspected none; but while the power of his friends over him seemed to have no limits, and really had none, in respect to those things which were of a nature to be yielded, no man, not the Roman Cato himself, was more inflexible on every point that touched, or only seemed to touch, integrity and honour. With him, it was not enough to be unsuspected; his bosom would have glowed like a furnace at its own whispers of reproach. Mere purity would have seemed to him below praise; and such were his habits and such his nature, that the pecuniary temptations, which many others can, only with great exertion and self-denial, resist, had no attractions for him.

He was very far from obstinate. Yet as his friends assailed his opinions with less profound thought than he had devoted to them, they were seldom shaken by discussion. He defended them, however, with as much mildness as force, and evinced that, if he did not yield, it was not for want of gentleness or modesty.

The tears that flow on this fond recital will never dry up. My heart, penetrated with the remembrance of the man, grows liquid as I write, and I could pour it out like water. I could weep too for my country, which, mournful as it is, does not know the half of its loss. It deeply laments, when it turns its eyes back, and sees what Hamilton *was;* but my soul stiffens with despair when I think what Hamilton *would have been.*

His social affections, and his private virtues, are not, however, so properly the object of public attention, as the conspicuous and commanding qualities that gave him his fame and influence in the world. It is not as Apollo, enchanting the shepherds with his lyre; it is as Hercules, treacherously slain, in the midst of his unfinished labours, leaving the world overrun with monsters, that we most deeply deplore him.

His early life we pass over — Though his heroic spirit in the army has furnished a theme that is dear to patriotism, and will be sacred to glory.

In all the different stations in which a life of active usefulness has placed him, we find him not more remarkably distinguished by the extent, than by the variety and versatility of his talents. In every place, he made it apparent, that no other man could have filled it so well, and, in times of critical importance, in which alone he desired employment, his services were justly deemed indispensable. As Secretary of the Treasury, his was the powerful spirit that presided over the Chaos —

> Confusion heard his voice, and wild uproar
> Stood ruled—

Indeed, in organizing the Federal Government in 1789, every man of either sense or candour will allow, the difficulty seemed greater than the first rate abilities could surmount. The event has shown that his abilities were greater than those difficulties. He surmounted them, and Washington's administration was the most wise and beneficent, the most prosperous, and ought to be the most popular, that ever was intrusted with the affairs of a nation. Great as was Washington's merit, much of it in plan, much in execution, will of course devolve upon his minister.

As a Lawyer, his comprehensive genius reached the principles of his profession; he compassed its extent, he fathomed its profound, perhaps even more familiarly and easily, than the ordinary rules of its practice. With most men, law is a trade; with him it was a science.

As a Statesman, he was not more distinguished by the great extent of his views, than by the caution with which he provided against impediments, and the watchfulness of his care, over right and the liberty of the subject. In none of the many revenue bills which he framed, though Committees reported them, is there to be found a single clause that savours of despotic power; not one that the sagest champions of law and liberty would, on that ground, hesitate to approve and adopt.

It is rare that a man who owes so much to nature descends to seek more from industry. But he seemed to depend on industry, as if nature had done nothing for him. His habits of investigation were very remarkable; his mind seemed to cling to his subject, till he had exhausted it. Hence the uncommon superiority of his reasoning powers, a superiority that seemed to be augmented from every source, and to be fortified by every auxiliary; learning, taste, wit, imagination, and eloquence. These were embellished and enforced by his temper and manners, by his fame and his virtues. It is difficult, in the midst of such various excellence, to say in what particular the effect of his greatness was most manifest. No man more promptly discerned truth, no man more clearly displayed it; it was not merely made visible, it seemed to come bright with illumination from his lips. But prompt and clear as he was, fervid as Demosthenes, like Cicero, full of resource, he was not less remarkable for the copiousness and completeness of his argument, that left little for cavil, and nothing for doubt. Some men take their strongest argument as a weapon, and use no other. But he left nothing to be inquired for more — nothing to be answered. He not only disarmed his adversaries of their pretexts and objections, but he stripped them of all excuse for having urged them: he confounded and subdued as well as convinced. He indemnified them, however, by making his discussion a complete map of his subject, so that his opponents might indeed feel ashamed of their mistakes, but they could not repeat them. In fact, it was no common effort, that could preserve a really able antagonist from becoming his convert. For, the truth, which his researches so distinctly presented to the understanding of others, was rendered almost irresistibly commanding and impressive, by the love and reverence which, it was ever apparent, he profoundly cherished for it in his own. While patriotism glowed in his heart, wisdom blended, in his speech, her authority with her charms.

SUCH also is the character of his writings. Judiciously collected, they will be a public treasure.

No man ever more disdained duplicity, or carried *frankness* further than he. This gave to his political opponents some temporary advantages; and currency to some popular prejudices, which he would have *lived* down, if his death had not prematurely dispelled them. He knew that factions have ever in the end prevailed in free States, and as he saw no security, and who living can see any adequate, against the destruction of that liberty which he loved, and for which he was ever ready to devote his life, he spoke at all times according to his anxious forebodings, and his enemies interpreted all that he said according to the supposed interest of their party.

But he ever extorted confidence even when he most provoked opposition. It was impossible to deny that he was a patriot — and such a patriot, seeking neither popularity nor office, without artifice, without meanness, the best Romans in their best days would have admitted to citizenship, and to the Consulate. Virtue so rare, so pure, so bold, by its very purity and excellence, inspired suspicion, as a prodigy. His enemies judged of him by themselves. So splendid and arduous were his services, they could not find it in *their* hearts to believe that they were disinterested.

Unparalleled as they were, they were nevertheless no otherwise requited than by the applause of all good men, and by his own enjoyment of the spectacle of that national prosperity and consideration, which was the effect of them. After facing calumny and triumphantly surmounting an unrelenting persecution, he retired from office with clean, though empty hands, as rich as reputation and an unblemished integrity could make him.

Some have plausibly, though erroneously, inferred from the great extent of his abilities, that his ambition was inordinate. This is a mistake. Such men as have a painful consciousness that their stations happen to be far more exalted than their talents, are generally the most ambitious. Hamilton, on the contrary, though he had many competitors, had no rivals; for he did not thirst for power, nor would he, as it was well known, descend to office. Of course he suffered no pain from envy when bad men rose, though he felt anxiety for the public. He was perfectly content and at ease in private life. Of what was he ambitious? not of wealth. No man held it cheaper. Was it of popularity? That weed of the dunghill, he knew, when rankest, was nearest to withering. There is no doubt, that, being conscious of his powers, he desired glory, which to most men is too inaccessible to be an object of desire. But feeling his own force, and that he was tall enough to reach the top of Pindus or of Helicon, he longed to deck his brow with the wreath of immortality. A vulgar ambition could as little comprehend as satisfy his views; he thirsted only for that fame that virtue would not blush to confer, nor time to convey to the end of his course.

The only ordinary distinction to which we confess he did aspire was military, and for that, in the event of a foreign war, he would have been solicitous. He undoubtedly discovered the predominance of a soldier's feelings; and all that is honour, in the character of a soldier, was at home in his heart. His early education was in the camp; there the first fervours of his genius were poured forth, and his earliest and most cordial friendships formed. There he became enamoured of glory, and was admitted to its embrace.

Those who knew him best, and especially in the army, will believe that if occasion had called him forth, he was qualified beyond any man of the age, to display the talents of a great General.

It may be very long before our country will want such military talents. It will probably be much longer before it will again possess them.

Alas! the great man, who was at all times so much the ornament of our country, and so exclusively fitted in its extremity to be its champion, is withdrawn to a purer and more tranquil region.

We are left to endless labours and unavailing regrets.

> Such honours Ilion to her hero paid,
> And peaceful slept the mighty Hector's shade.

Our Troy has lost her Hector.

The most substantial glory of a country is in its virtuous great men. Its prosperity will depend on its docility to learn from their example. That nation is fated to ignominy and servitude, for which such men have lived in vain. Power may be seized by a nation that is yet barbarous, and wealth may be enjoyed by one that it finds, or renders sordid; the one is the gift and the sport of accident, and the other is the sport of power. Both are mutable, and have passed away without leaving behind them any other memorial than ruins that offend taste, and traditions that baffle conjecture. But the glory of Greece is imperishable, or will last as long as learning itself, which is its monument. It strikes an everlasting root, and bears perennial blossoms on its grave. The name of Hamilton would not have dishonoured Greece in the age of Aristides. May Heaven, the guardian of our liberty, grant, that our country may be fruitful of Hamiltons and faithful to their glory.

TRIBUTE OF RESPECT.

At a general meeting of the inhabitants of Geneva, at Powell's Hotel, in the evening of the 2d inst. agreeably to notice, for the purpose of uniting with their fellow-citizens at large, in expressing their unfeigned sorrow and regret, at the untimely death of *General Alexander Hamilton*, and the great loss this country has sustained in the death of that invaluable man—

DANIEL W. LEWIS, Esquire,

was called to the chair—

Who, in a solemn and impressive manner, opened the meeting; and, in a few observations, recapitulated the Talents, Patriotism, and Virtues, of the deceased, when the following resolutions were unanimously adopted.

THAT this Meeting feel the most sensible grief at the death of General Hamilton, and with their fellow-citizens throughout the union, deplore and lament the event, as a great national loss.

THAT this Meeting are impressed with a just sense of the merit attached to the character of the deceased, acquired by his distinguished and highly honourable services rendered his country as a Soldier — his pre-eminent display of talents and eloquence as a Statesman and Lawyer — and his exalted principles of honour and integrity, as a private Citizen, do agree, as a tribute of respect due to his memory, to wear a Crape on the left arm, for thirty days. — And, as a further tribute of respect, That Mr. Gordon, Mr. Weisner, and Mr. Heslop, be appointed a committee on behalf of this Meeting, to wait on the Rev. Mr. Chapman, and request the favour of him to preach a Sermon to-morrow afternoon adapted to the occasion; and the inhabitants of the Village are requested to meet at 4 o'clock in the afternoon, to form a solemn procession to the Meeting-House.

Wm. H. CUYLER, *Secretary.*

Agreeably to the above arrangements, the inhabitants of the Village met, and formed a procession to the house of worship, when the Rev. Mr. Chapman delivered a Sermon on the above occasion, from Hosea, Chap. 4th, part of verse 3d — "*Therefore shall the land mourn.*"

END OF NO. V.

AN ORATION,

COMMEMORATIVE OF THE LATE

Major-General Alexander Hamilton;

PRONOUNCED BEFORE

The New-York State Society

of the Cincinnati,

ON TUESDAY, THE 31ST JULY, 1804.

BY J. M. MASON, D. D.

PASTOR OF THE FIRST ASSOCIATE REFORMED CHURCH IN THE CITY OF NEW-YORK.

Quis desiderio sit pudor aut modus
Tam cari capitis? — Hor.

Φεῦ ὦ ἀγαθὴ καὶ πιστὴ ψυχὴ, οἴχῃ δὴ ἀπολιπῶν ἡμᾶς. — Xenoph.

AT a Meeting of the Society of the Cincinnati, held at the Federal Hall in the City of New-York, on Tuesday, 31st July, 1804;

RESOLVED UNANIMOUSLY, That the respectful Thanks of this Society be presented to the Rev. Dr. JOHN M. MASON, for the very eloquent, impressive, and instructive ORATION, delivered by him this day, at their request, on the ever to be lamented Death of their President, Major-General ALEXANDER HAMILTON; and that a Committee be appointed to wait on him and request that he will be pleased to furnish them with a copy for the press.

RESOLVED UNANIMOUSLY, That the present Committee of Arrangement wait on the Rev. Dr. JOHN M. MASON, with a copy of these resolutions.

Extract from the Minutes,

W. POPHAM, *Secretary.*

FUNERAL ORATION.

SAD, my fellow-citizens, are the recollections and forebodings which the present solemnities force upon the mind. Five years have not elapsed since your tears flowed for the Father of your Country, and you are again assembled to shed them over her eldest Son. No, it is not an illusion — would to God it were: Your eyes behold it: the Urn which bore the ashes of WASHINGTON, is followed by the Urn which bears the ashes of HAMILTON. Cruel privation! — But I forbear. God's "way is "in the sea, and his path in the great waters, and his foot- "steps are not known." It is not for mortals to repine, much less to arraign. Our HAMILTON is removed; and we have nothing left but to recal his image; to gather up his maxims, and to profit by our affliction. Accompany me, therefore, to a short retrospect. I feel that I shall not justify an appointment too imposing to be declined. Your own hearts must supply my deficiency. I aspire to nothing more than a faint outline of the man whom you loved.

PRESAGES of his future eminence were evolved by the first buddings of intellect in ALEXANDER HAMILTON. The course of the boy, like that of the man, was ardent, rapid, and beyond the reach of his contemporaries. History will hereafter relate that he was numbered among Statesmen at an age when in others the rudiments of character are scarcely visible. In the contest with Great-Britain, which called forth every talent and every passion, his juvenile pen asserted the claims of the colonies, against writers from whom it would derogate to say that they were merely respectable. An unknown antagonist, whose thrust was neither to be repelled nor parried, excited inquiry; and when he began to be discovered, the effect was apparently so disproportioned to the cause, that his papers were ascribed to a statesman who then held a happy sway in the councils of his country, who has since rendered her the most essential services; and who still lives to adorn her name.* But the truth could not long be concealed. The powers of HAMILTON created their own evidence; and America saw, with astonishment, a lad of seventeen in the rank of her advocates, at a time when her advocates were patriots and sages. A distinction thus nobly acquired, and ably maintained, was a pledge to the commonwealth, which he lost no time in redeeming. His first step, from the college, was into a military post; his second into the family and confidence of WASHINGTON. Here he had opportunities of studying a man, from whom no other man was too great to learn; of analyzing those rare qualities which met in his character; and of nourishing his own magnanimity by free communication with the magnanimity of his chief. His sound understanding, his comprehensive views, his promptitude, application, and patience, would have endeared him to a man less discriminating than WASHINGTON; but to him they were inestimable, and they speedily sunk the patron in the friend. The pair became inseparable. While others were indulging in wonted gaiety, they were closeted on matters of state; and the pensive brow of the youth was often the first intimation of serious design in the veteran.

* John Jay, Esq.

It was impossible for such a pupil, in such a school, not to be conspicuous. The materials furnished by WASHINGTON's experience; by his consummate prudence; by the disclosure of his plans, and of the springs of national operations, fostered the genius of HAMILTON, and fitted him for command. His agency in the correspondence of the Commander in Chief, and in directing the movements of the army, is for the research of his biographer. I pass over his personal valour, not only because it never was disputed; but because the possession of it, as being one of the most common of military attributes, is not so much the praise of a soldier, as the want of it is his infamy. But be it remembered with pride, that he was as humane as he was brave. He knew how to storm an enemy's intrenchments, but not how to sacrifice a suppliant. His gentleness assuaged martial rigour; nor was his sword polluted by a drop of blood wantonly or carelessly shed.

THE capture of Lord Cornwallis having secured our independence, there was nothing to protract the war, but a few measures proper to save appearances, and to prepare for acceding, with decorum, to preliminaries of peace. It became, of course, a subject of solicitude to reflecting young men who had no profession but that of arms, how they should procure an honourable subsistence, and be useful to the community, when that profession should be superseded. Among these was HAMILTON. Encumbered with a family, destitute of funds, and having no inducement to continue in the army, he sheathed his sword, and, at the age of twenty-five, applied to the study of the Law.

To most men, sudden alterations of habit are seldom advantageous, often ruinous. HAMILTON they did but introduce to an acquaintance with his own inexhaustible mind. Hardly had he exchanged the camp for the bar, when he burst forth in the lustre of a civilian; and gave a promise which he more than fulfilled, of excelling in jurisprudence, as he had excelled in war.

But it was not for HAMILTON to detach his private pursuits from the public welfare. Scenes were about to open in which it would need his resource and his energy. The war of independence had terminated gloriously; the states had risen to their natural position; their career of prosperity had commenced, but their struggles were not over. Resentments, jealousies, and the farce of an *advising* government, kept them in jeopardy. That foresight, moderation, and firmness; that comprehension of the public interest, and of the means of promoting it; that zeal, and vigilance, and integrity, which were indispensable to our safety, the inspiration of God had assembled in the soul of HAMILTON. To many who now hear me it is familiar, that after the conclusion of peace, some of our citizens, impelled by their temper, their cupidity, or both, were meditating violence against the property and persons of all who had remained in this city during the war. The generous HAMILTON revolted. No consideration of private friendship or hazard could prevail with him to connive at faithlessness and revenge. He remonstrated against a scheme of which the policy was as false, as the spirit was malignant. His voice was authority, for it was honour and truth. The public listened, and the infatuation was at an end.*

* On this subject it would be less a compliment to mention, than an injury to omit, the name of his Excellency George Clinton, Esq. then Governor of the State; whose honourable, independent, and successful

To these agitations succeeded a more perplexing difficulty. The confederation, framed under the pressure of common danger, proved unequal to its object whenever that pressure was removed. Thirteen republics, with an internal organization which commanded their whole moral and physical force; connected by a fictitious tie under a head without a single effective power, afforded a spectacle of which it is hard to say, whether it was more ludicrous or melancholy. Such a condition of things could not last. The very first occurrence which should put the will of congress at issue with the will of one of the larger states, would have dissolved the phantom; and shown America to be, what the discerning at home and abroad already perceived her to be, in theory, a nation; in fact, a number of rival and hostile sovereignties. The evils to be apprehended from such a conflict were alarming; and they were approaching with no less certainty, than it is certain that the principles of human action are not to be altered, nor suspended by compact. The failure of a request from Congress for permission to levy a small duty upon imports, was hastening a crisis which the mighty mind of HAMILTON proposed to avert. With the express intention of making an effort to retrieve our affairs by establishing an efficient general government, did he consent to be nominated as a candidate for the legislature of this state. The design was magnanimous. It embraced the only expedient to prevent our ruin; but it was confided to a few chosen friends. For such was the national inexperience, and the popular jealousy, that the least suspicion of his purpose would have blasted his reputation as an enemy to freedom. Oh, HAMILTON! equally pure and disinterested

exertions to restrain our citizens, cannot be remembered but with respect and veneration.

were all thy plans, though often misunderstood and calumniated! And now, when there is no more room for suspicion, let his country in judging of them, not forget, that the very measure which, at first, she would bitterly have execrated, has been her salvation. Yes, it is indubitable, that the original germ out of which has grown up her unexampled prosperity, was in the bosom of HAMILTON. From the abortive attempt of Congress already mentioned, proceeded a commercial convention; and to the report of that body, which, as he foresaw, was unable to extricate the nation, do we owe the Federal Convention. Here, Americans, was the constellation of your heroes and your statesmen. Here your WASHINGTON presided, and your HAMILTON shone. What weight the first of these names added to every thing which received its sanction, and what a conciliating charm it diffused through the states, you need not be informed. But you ought not to be ignorant, that the benefit arising from the signature of WASHINGTON substantiates a claim on your gratitude to HAMILTON; as it was the advice of the latter previously consulted, which persuaded the former to accept a seat in the convention. A prudent secrecy covers the transactions of that august assembly. But could the veil be drawn aside, you would hear the youth of thirty fascinating, with his eloquence, the collective wisdom of the states; and instructing the hoary patriot in the recondite science of government. You would observe all the emotions of his manly heart occupying, in turn, his expressive features; and see, through the window in his breast, every anxiety, every impulse, every thought, directed to your happiness.

THE result is in your hands: it is in your national existence. Not such, indeed, as HAMILTON wished, but such as he could obtain, and as the states would ratify, is the federal constitution. His ideas of a government which should elevate the character, preserve the unity, and perpetuate the liberties of America, went beyond the provisions of that instrument. Accustomed to view men as they are; and to judge of what they will be, from what they ever have been, he distrusted any political order which admits the baneful charity of supposing them to be what they ought to be. He knew how averse they are from even wholesome restraint; how obsequious to flattery; how easily deceived by misrepresentation: how partial, how vehement, how capricious. He knew that vanity, the love of distinction, is inseparable from man; that if it be not turned into a channel useful to the government, it will force a channel for itself; and if cut off from other egress, will issue in the most corrupt of all aristocracies — the aristocracy of money. He knew, that an extensive territory, a progressive population, an expanding commerce, diversified climate, and soil, and manners, and interest, must generate faction; must interfere with foreign views, and present emergencies requiring, in the general organization, much tone and promptitude. A strong government, therefore; that is, a government stable and vigorous; adequate to all the forms of national exigency; and furnished with the principles of self-preservation, was undoubtedly his preference; and he preferred it because he conscientiously believed it to be necessary. A system which he would have entirely approved, would probably keep in their places those little men who aspire to be great; would withdraw much fuel from the passions of the multitude; would diminish the materials which the worthless employ for their own aggrandizement; would crown peace at home with respectability abroad; but would never infringe the liberty of an honest man. From his profound acquaintance with mankind, and his devotion to all that good society holds dear, sprang his apprehensions for the existing constitution. Convinced that the natural tendency of things is to an encroachment by the states on the union; that their encroachments will be formidable as they augment their wealth and population, and, consequently, that the vigour of the general government will be impaired in a very near proportion with the increase of its difficulties; he anticipated the day when it should perish in the conflict of local interest and of local pride. The divine mercy grant that his prediction may not be verified!

But whatever fears he entertained for the ultimate safety of the Federal constitution; it is, in every respect, so preferable to the old confederation, and its rejection would have been so extremely hazardous, that he exerted all his talents and influence in its support. In the papers signed PUBLIUS, which compress the experience of ages, and pour original light on the science of government, his genius has left a manual for the future statesman. And they will be read with deeper interest when it is considered that, eloquent and powerful as they are, they were written under the pressure of business, amidst the conversation of friends, and the interrogatories of clients. Alas! the spirit which dictated them is fled; the hand which penned them moulders in death!

His voice co-operated with his pen. In the Convention of this state, which met to deliberate on the Federal constitution, he was always heard with awe, perhaps with conviction; though not always with success. But when the crisis arrived — when a vote was to determine whether

New-York should retain or relinquish her place in the union; and preceding occurrences made it probable that she would choose the worst part of the alternative, HAMILTON arose in redoubled strength. He argued, he remonstrated, he entreated, he warned, he painted, till apathy itself was moved, and the most relentless of human things, a preconcerted majority, was staggered and broken. Truth was again victorious, and New-York enrolled herself under the Federal standard.

THE government happily erected, was now to be organized. Every eye fixed upon WASHINGTON for the first magistrate. He knew it, and hesitated. The competition between his love of retirement, his former resolutions, and the new state of affairs, held him in painful suspense. But the judgment of HAMILTON preponderated, and he yielded to the public wish.

THAT faithful adviser, whom he had consulted upon every question of moment, and who never gave him an unsound advice, could not be omitted in the original administration. The department best suited to him, because the most arduous, was the Treasury. He had already passed from the Warrior into the Jurist, and he was now to appear in the new and very different character of a Financier. A losing commerce, a famished agriculture, an empty purse, and prostrate credit, would have overwhelmed the ordinary man; but they only brought into action the resources of HAMILTON. His plans for redeeming the reputation of the country, by satisfying her creditors; and for combining with the government such a monied interest as might facilitate its operations, were strenuously opposed. But as it is easier to cavil than to refute, to complain than to amend, the opposition failed. The effect was electrical. Commerce revived; the ploughshare glittered; property recovered its value; credit was established; revenue created; the treasury filled.

THIS great fiscal revolution enriched numbers who held a large amount of the public paper, purchased at a season when the unpromising state of the public faith had set it afloat in the market at a most ignoble price. None could have fairer opportunities of acquiring a princely fortune, than the financier himself. So inviting was the occasion, and the disposition to profit by it so little at variance with the common estimate of honourable gain, that few supposed it possible to resist the temptation. The fact being presumed, every petty politician erected himself into a critic; while the gazettes, the streets, the polls of election, resounded with the millions amassed by the Secretary. It is natural that the idolaters of gold should treat the contempt of it as a chimera: But gold was not the idol of HAMILTON. He had formerly relinquished his own claims to compensation for military services, that obloquy might not breathe an impeachment of his motives in espousing the claims of his brother officers.* And from this proud eminence

* Being a member of Congress, while the question of the commutation of the half pay of the army for a sum in gross was in debate, delicacy, and a desire to be useful to the army, by removing the idea of his having an interest in the question, induced him to write to the Secretary of War, and relinquish his claim to half pay; which, or the equivalent, he accordingly never received. Neither did he ever apply for the lands allowed by the United States to officers of his rank. It is true, that having served through the latter periods of the war on the general staff of the United States, and not in the line of this state, he could not claim the allowance as a matter of course. But having before the war resided in this state, and having entered the military career at the head of a company of Artillery

which he then ascended, he was not now to be seduced by the attractions of lucre. Exquisitely delicate toward official character, he touched none of the advantages which he put within the reach of others; he vested not a dollar in the public funds.

ALTHOUGH his particular province was the TREASURY, his genius pervaded the whole administration; and in those critical events which crowded each other, had a peculiar influence upon its measures. The French revolution, which our fondness mistook for the birth of virtuous freedom, stood before him, from the beginning, in that hideous form which it has since unmasked. Not to be duped by hollow pretences, he was active in arresting the course of an insolent minister: and not to be biassed by popular frenzy, he secured that dignified ground to which the United States were led by the proclamation of neutrality. Without his aid, great WASHINGTON himself might have been borne down by the torrent, and the nation implicated in war to gratify the resentment and ambition of France.

INTERNAL embarrassment soon added fresh honours to HAMILTON as a statesman. The western insurrection, which had rejected the condescending proposals of government, was to be quelled by force. A more serious question had not occupied the cabinet, as nothing had hitherto occurred to try the strength of the national arm. It was now to be ascertained how far the turbulent might trifle with the law; and what reliance they might place upon armed opposition. Incalculable consequences hung

raised for the particular defence of this state, he had better pretensions to the allowance than others to whom it was actually made. Yet has it not been extended to him.

upon the precedent. Feeble measures would have surrendered the peace, perhaps the life of the union; but feeble measures were contemplated. That timidity which shrinks from decision; that economy which accounts every thing less precious than money; and that covert treason which favoured the rebellion, would have ordered out a detachment that might have been met and defeated.

THE penetration of HAMILTON was not to be eluded, nor his firmness to be shaken, by any argument in support of so dangerous an experiment. " If you wish," said he, " to maintain the authority of the laws; to prevent " the repetition of similar outrages; to spare your treas- " ure and your blood; let the insurgents, let the conti- " nent see, that it is never to admit of a doubt whether " the national will shall be obeyed or not. Teach them " this lesson by employing a force which shall put resist- " ance out of the question." This sage and humane policy was adopted by WASHINGTON; and the rebellion disappeared without effusion of blood.

AFTER the restoration of order, Mr. HAMILTON remained but a short time in office. His numerous services gave him, perhaps, a right to retire when the state might be safely intrusted to other hands. But one reason of his retreat deserves particular notice, because it involves a mischievous and disreputable principle. A general error in popular systems is a frugality which computes nothing but pence. The affairs of a nation, however, cannot be ably conducted without able and independent men. But such men, in a country where the demand for active talent is greater than the supply, will always hold their fortunes in their own hand: nor are we to expect that they will submit to the toils and responsibility of public office with a support utterly disproportioned both to their station and their means of providing for themselves. No people is in jeopardy from the liberality of their civil list: But when this is niggardly, able men withdraw in succession, and the state falls, at length, into the hands of the weak or the wicked, whose want of capacity, or of integrity, squanders on one occasion, the public revenue, and on another, overloads it with the expenses of war. The last of these consequences God forbid we should experience; the first was exemplified in the history of HAMILTON. He entered into public service with property of his own, the well-earned reward of professional talent; he continued in it, till his little funds were dissipated; and left it, to get bread for a suffering family. It was surely enough that he had impoverished himself while he was enriching the commonwealth; but it was beyond measure insulting to charge him, under such circumstances, with invading the public purse. Nobody believed the charge; and least of all, the slanderers who brought it. But WASHINGTON was vilified, and how should HAMILTON escape! The virtuous saw, with regret, that he stooped to repel it; and with anguish, that in regard to a private aberration, his defence contained a disclosure of which they admired the ingenuousness, but deplored the occasion, while they wept over a spot in a blaze of excellence.

LARGE and lucrative practice at the bar promised to replace his pecuniary sacrifices in official life. But a new distress of his country drew him again from his professional engagements. Our remonstrances against the injuries committed by France, had proved unavailing; and her rude and humiliating requisitions had fired the national spirit. Little was to be expected from the generosity, and less from the rectitude, of a government framed upon the maxims of the new philosophy. Tribute or the sword, was the only choice of the States, and it would have been a libel on the war of independence to have hesitated a moment. A provisional army, with WASHINGTON at their head, was summoned into the field: but the condition on which he suspended the acceptance of his own commission was, that HAMILTON should be his associate. The end of this stipulation could not be misunderstood. He not only designed to have his age relieved from some heavy cares by his younger friend; but, in the event of his own decease, to leave the sword of America in the hands of a man, whom nothing could overreach, nothing intimidate, nothing corrupt.

SUBSEQUENT adjustment of our dispute with the French Republic, was accompanied with the discharge of the provisional army, and with HAMILTON's second return to his profession. Here, unwearied in diligence, and unrivalled in fame, he filled up the residue, (ah, too transient!) of his invaluable days. But, as you have truly been told, though he had withdrawn from public life, he was not an hour absent from the public service. It did not belong to a man absorbed in his country's welfare, to look with indifference on the course of her affairs. Office he wanted none. None in the gift of the nation would have moved him from his purpose. He reserved himself for crises which, he feared, are approaching; such crises, especially, as may affect the integrity of the union. How he was alarmed by every thing which pointed at its dissolution; how indignant were his feelings and language on that ungracious topic; how stern and steady his hostility to every influence which only leaned toward the project, they will attest with whom he was in habits of communication. In every shape, it encountered his reprobation as unworthy of a statesman, as fatal to America, and desirable to the desperate alone. One of his primary objects was to consolidate the efforts of good men in retarding a calamity which, after all, they may be unable to avert; but which no partial nor temporary policy should induce them to accelerate. To these sentiments must be traced his hatred of continental factions; his anxiety for the federal constitution, although, in his judgment, too slight for the pressure it has to sustain; his horror of every attempt to sap its foundation or loosen its fabric; his zeal to consecrate it in the affections of his fellow-citizens, that if it fall at last, they may be pure from the guilt of its overthrow — an overthrow, which may be accomplished in an hour, but of which the woes may be entailed upon ages to come.

WITH such dignified policy he joined the most intense application to his professional duties. But the description of these is not my province. How he resolved the most intricate cases; how he pursued general principles through their various modifications; how he opened the fountains of justice; how he revered the rights of property; how he signalized himself in protecting the defenceless; how judges, and jurors, and counsel, and audience, hung on his accents; let them declare who have intrusted their fortunes to his hand: Let them declare who have wondered that any man should be thought great while HAMILTON appeared at the American bar.

BUT enumerations were endless. He was born to be great. Whoever was second, HAMILTON must be first. To his stupendous and versatile mind no investigation was difficult — no subject presented which he did not illuminate. Superiority, in some particular, belongs to thousands. Pre-eminence, in whatever he chose to undertake, was the prerogative of HAMILTON. No fixed criterion could be applied to his talents. Often has their display been supposed to have reached the limit of human effort, and the judgment stood firm till set aside by himself. When a cause of new magnitude required new exertion, he rose, he towered, he soared; surpassing himself, as he surpassed others. Then was nature tributary to his eloquence! Then was felt his despotism over the heart! Touching, at his pleasure, every string of pity or terror, of indignation or grief; he melted, he soothed, he roused, he agitated; alternately gentle as the dews, and awful as the thunder. Yet, great as he was in the eyes of the world, he was greater in the eyes of those with whom he was most conversant. The greatness of most men, like objects seen through a mist, diminishes with the distance: but HAMILTON, like a tower seen afar off under a clear sky, rose in grandeur and sublimity with every step of approach. Familiarity with him was the parent of veneration. Over these matchless talents Probity threw her brightest lustre. Frankness, suavity, tenderness, benevolence, breathed through their exercise. And to his family! — but he is gone. — That noble heart beats no more: that eye of fire is dimmed; and sealed are those oracular lips. Americans, the serenest beam of your glory is extinguished in the tomb!

FATHERS, friends, countrymen! the death of HAMILTON is no common affliction. The loss of distinguished men is, at all times, a calamity; but the loss of such a man, at such a time, and in the very meridian of his usefulness, is singularly portentous. When WASHINGton was taken, Hamilton was left — but Hamilton is taken, and we have no Washington. We have not such another man to die! Washington and Hamilton in five years! — Bereaved America! Thou art languishing beneath the divine displeasure. Let this truth awfully impress my hearers, that when the Almighty God is about to "shake terribly the earth;" when he has bidden scourge to follow scourge, and vengeance to press on vengeance, one of his means is to deprive a nation of their ablest men. Thus bereft of counsel, their affairs run into confusion, and bring forth misery. I invent nothing; I only repeat the admonition of holy writ: "For behold the Lord, the Lord of hosts doth take "away the mighty man, and the man of war, the judge, "and the prophet, and the prudent, and the ancient, the "captain of fifty, and the honourable man, and the coun- "sellor, and the cunning artificer, and the eloquent ora- "tor." The disastrous consequences are, impotent governors, and ruthless anarchy. For the prophet continues, "I will give children to be their princes, and babes shall "rule over them. And the people shall be oppressed, "every one by another, and every one by his neighbour; "the child shall behave himself proudly against the an- "cient, and the base against the honourable."

Fathers, friends, countrymen! the grave of Hamilton speaks. It charges me to remind you that he fell a victim, not to disease nor accident; not to the fortune of glorious warfare; but, how shall I utter it? to a custom which has no origin but superstition, no aliment but depravity, no reason but in madness. Alas! that he should thus expose his precious life. This was his error. A thousand bursting hearts reiterate, this *was* his error. Shall I apologize? I am forbidden by his living protestations, by his dying regrets, by his wasted blood. Shall a solitary act into which he was betrayed and dragged, have the authority of a precedent? The plea is precluded by the long decisions of his understanding, by the principles of his conscience, and by the reluctance of his heart. Ah! when will our morals be purified, and an imaginary honour cease to cover the most pestilent of human passions? My appeal is to military men. Your honour is sacred. Listen. Is it honourable to enjoy the esteem of the wise and good? The wise and good turn with disgust from the man who lawlessly aims at his neighbour's life. Is it honourable to serve your country? That man cruelly injures her, who, from private pique, calls his fellow-citizen into the dubious field. Is fidelity honourable? That man forswears his faith, who turns against the bowels of his countrymen, weapons put into his hand for their defence. Are generosity, humanity, sympathy, honourable? That man is superlatively base, who mingles the tears of the widow and orphan, with the blood of a husband and father. Do refinement, and courtesy, and benignity, entwine with the laurels of the brave? The blot is yet to be wiped from the soldier's name, that he cannot treat his brother with the decorum of a gentleman, unless the pistol or the dagger be every moment at his heart. Let the votaries of honour now look at their deeds. Let them compare their doctrine with this horrible comment. Ah! what avails it to a distracted nation that HAMILTON was murdered for a punctilio of honour? My flesh shivers! Is this, indeed, our state of society? Are transcendent worth and talent to be a capital indictment before the tribunal of ambition? Is the Angel of Death to record, for sanguinary retribution, every word which the collision of political opinion may extort from a political man?

Are integrity and candour to be at the mercy of the assassin? And systematic crime to trample under foot, or smite into the grave, all that is yet venerable in our humbled land? My countrymen, the land is defiled with blood unrighteously shed. Its cry, disregarded on earth, has gone up to the throne of God; and this day does our punishment reveal our sin. It is time for us to awake. The voice of moral virtue, the voice of domestic alarm, the voice of the fatherless and widow, the voice of a nation's wrong, the voice of HAMILTON's blood, the voice of impending judgment, calls for a remedy. At this hour Heaven's high reproof is sounding from Maine to Georgia, and from the shores of the Atlantic to the banks of the Mississippi. If we refuse obedience, every drop of blood spilled in single combat, will lie at our door, and will be recompensed when our cup is full. We have, then, our choice, either to coerce iniquity, or prepare for desolation; and in the mean time, to make our nation, though infant in years, yet mature in vice, the scorn and the abhorrence of civilized man!

FATHERS, friends, countrymen! the dying breath of HAMILTON recommended to you the Christian's hope. His single testimony outweighs all the cavils of the sciolist, and all the jeers of the profane. Who will venture to pronounce a fable, that doctrine of "life and immortality," which his profound and irradiating mind embraced as the truth of God? When you are to die, you will find no source of peace but in the faith of Jesus. Cultivate for your present repose and your future consolation, what our departed friend declared to be the support of his expiring moments:—"A tender reli-"ance on the mercies of the Almighty, through the "merits of the Lord Jesus Christ."

HAMILTON! we will cherish thy memory, we will embalm thy fame! Fare thee well, thou unparalleled man, farewell — for ever!